BRUCE SPRINGSTEEN

★ ★

POP CULTURE LEGENDS

BRUCE SPRINGSTEEN

★ ★

RON FRANKL

CHELSEA HOUSE PUBLISHERS

New York ★ Philadelphia

CHELSEA HOUSE PUBLISHERS

EDITORIAL DIRECTOR Richard Rennert
EXECUTIVE MANAGING EDITOR Karyn Gullen Browne
COPY CHIEF Robin James
PICTURE EDITOR Adrian G. Allen
ART DIRECTOR Robert Mitchell
MANUFACTURING DIRECTOR Gerald Levine
PRODUCTION COORDINATOR Marie Claire Cebrián-Ume

Pop Culture Legends
SENIOR EDITOR Kathy Kuhtz Campbell
SERIES DESIGN Basia Niemczyc

Staff for BRUCE SPRINGSTEEN
ASSOCIATE EDITOR Martin Schwabacher
EDITORIAL ASSISTANT Kelsey Goss
PICTURE RESEARCHER Lisa Kirchner
COVER ILLUSTRATION Daniel Mark Duffy

First Printing

1 3 5 7 9 8 6 4 2

Library of Congress Cataloging-in-Publication Data

Frankl, Ron.
Bruce Springsteen/Ron Frankl.
p. cm.—(Pop culture legends)
Includes bibliographical references and index.
Summary: Describes the life of the popular rock musician, singer, and songwriter Bruce Springsteen.
ISBN 0-7910-2327-3
      0-7910-2352-4 (pbk.)
1. Springsteen, Bruce—Juvenile literature. 2. Rock musicians—United States—Biography—Juvenile literature. [1. Springsteen, Bruce. 2. Musicians. 3. Rock music.] I. Title. II. Series.
ML3930.S72F7 1994   93-1850
782.42166'092   CIP
[B]   AC MN

FRONTISPIECE:
Bruce Springsteen performs before an American flag at the Los Angeles Memorial Coliseum in September 1985.

Contents ★ ★ ★ ★ ★ ★ ★ ★ ★ ★ ★ ★ ★ ★ ★ ★ ★ ★

A Reflection of Ourselves—*Leeza Gibbons*   7

★ 1   "Blinded by the Light"   11

★ 2   "Growin' Up"   17

★ 3   "Backstreets"   29

★ 4   "Thundercrack"   39

★ 5   "Thunder Road"   51

★ 6   "The E Street Shuffle"   63

★ 7   "The Promised Land"   73

★ 8   "Point Blank"   83

★ 9   "Glory Days"   99

★ 10   "Better Days"   113

Discography   122

Further Reading   123

Chronology   124

Index   126

A Reflection of Ourselves

Leeza Gibbons

I ENJOY A RARE PERSPECTIVE on the entertainment industry. From my window on popular culture, I can see all that sizzles and excites. I have interviewed legends who have left us, such as Bette Davis and Sammy Davis, Jr., and have brushed shoulders with the names who have caused a commotion with their sheer outrageousness, like Boy George and Madonna. Whether it's by nature or by design, pop icons generate interest, and I think they are a mirror of who we are at any given time.

Who are *your* heroes and heroines, the people you most admire? Outside of your own family and friends, to whom do you look for inspiration and guidance, as examples of the type of person you would like to be as an adult? How do we decide who will be the most popular and influential members of our society?

You may be surprised by your answers. According to recent polls, you will probably respond much differently than your parents or grandparents did to the same questions at the same age. Increasingly, world leaders such as Winston Churchill, John F. Kennedy, Franklin D. Roosevelt, and evangelist Billy Graham have been replaced by entertainers, athletes, and popular artists as the individuals whom young people most respect and admire. In surveys taken during each of the past 15 years, for example, General Norman Schwarzkopf was the only world leader chosen as the number-one hero among high school students. Other names on the elite list joined by General Schwarzkopf included Paula Abdul, Michael Jackson, Michael Jordan, Eddie Murphy, Burt Reynolds, and Sylvester Stallone.

More than 30 years have passed since Canadian sociologist Marshall McLuhan first taught us the huge impact that the electronic media has had on how we think, learn, and understand—as well as how we choose our heroes. In the 1960s, Pop artist Andy Warhol predicted that there would soon come a time when every American would be famous for 15 minutes. But if it is easier today to achieve Warhol's 15 minutes of fame, it is also much harder to hold on to it. Reputations are often ruined as quickly as they are made.

And yet, there remain those artists and performers who continue to inspire and instruct us in spite of changes in world events, media technology, or popular tastes. Even in a society as fickle and fast moving as our own, there are still those performers whose work and reputation endure, pop culture legends who inspire an almost religious devotion from their fans.

Why do the works and personalities of some artists continue to fascinate us while others are so quickly forgotten? What, if any, qualities do they share that enable them to have such power over our lives? There are no easy answers to these questions. The artists and entertainers profiled in this series often have little more in common than the enormous influence that each of them has had on our lives.

Some offer us an escape. Artists such as actress Marilyn Monroe, comedian Groucho Marx, and writer Stephen King have used glamour, humor, or fantasy to help us escape from our everyday lives. Others present us with images that are all too recognizable. The uncompromising realism of actor and director Charlie Chaplin and folk singer Bob Dylan challenges us to confront and change the things in our world that most disturb us.

Some offer us friendly, reassuring experiences. The work of animator Walt Disney and late-night talk show host Johnny Carson, for example, provides us with a sense of security and continuity in a changing world. Others shake us up. The best work of composer John Lennon and actor James Dean will always inspire their fans to question and reevaluate the world in which they live.

It is also hard to predict the kind of life that a pop culture legend will lead, or how he or she will react to fame. Popular singers Michael Jackson

and Prince carefully guard their personal lives from public view. Other performers, such as popular singer Madonna, enjoy putting their private lives before the public eye.

What these artists and entertainers do share, however, is the rare ability to capture and hold the public's imagination in a world dominated by mass media and disposable celebrity. In spite of their differences, each of them has somehow managed to achieve legendary status in a popular culture that values novelty and change.

The books in this series examine the lives and careers of these and other pop culture legends, and the society that places such great value on their work. Each book considers the extraordinary talent, the stubborn commitment, and the great personal sacrifice required to create work of enduring quality and influence in today's world.

As you read these books, ask yourself the following questions: How are the careers of these individuals shaped by their society? What role do they play in shaping the world? And what is it that so captivates us about their lives, their work, or the images they present?

Hopefully, by studying the lives and achievements of these pop culture legends, we will learn more about ourselves.

"Blinded by the Light"

AS BRUCE SPRINGSTEEN leaped from the stage into the audience, the huge crowd gave out a tremendous roar. It was May 26, 1978, and the city was Philadelphia, Pennsylvania, the third stop of a concert tour that would last seven months and 109 performances. It had been more than a year since Springsteen's last tour, but despite his absence from performing, his reputation as rock and roll's greatest live act had only grown.

Every concert on the tour would be sold out, usually within a few hours. This night's show at the Spectrum, an enormous basketball and ice hockey arena, was no exception. Some of his loyal fans had traveled hundreds of miles to experience the excitement. Many would attend concerts on more than one night—if they were lucky enough to get tickets.

On this May evening, Bruce Springsteen and the E Street Band were making a triumphant return to the Spectrum in Philadelphia. It was in Philadelphia that Springsteen had first built a huge following, and now he had come back to repay his devoted followers with a marathon concert. The crowd responded enthusiastically as saxophonist Clarence Clemons roared

---

At a concert in St. Paul, Minnesota, in June 1984, Bruce Springsteen displays the passion, charisma, and boundless energy that made him one of rock and roll's greatest stars.

into a rousing solo while the band belted out "Spirit in the Night," a longtime favorite among Springsteen fans. The high point of the song, about a crazy late-night party at a mythical place called Greasy Lake, came when Springsteen made his traditional jump into the first few rows of seats.

Usually the audience members would respond by looking on in awe or perhaps by patting Springsteen on the back. Occasionally Springsteen might pause to dance briefly with a young woman he chose from the crowd. Sometimes he would scamper back onto the stage at the conclusion of Clemons's stirring sax solo. Other nights, hemmed in by the audience, he would resume singing from the auditorium floor. As the audience surrounded the singer, he would seem to disappear while the concert's security staff attempted—usually unsuccessfully—to reclaim Springsteen from his adoring fans.

High in the mezzanine, several hundred feet from the action taking place in front of the stage, a fan searched for Springsteen somewhere in the first rows on the Spectrum floor. At most concerts Springsteen was not hard to find, as the crowd surged toward the singer and the spotlights pinpointed him among the outstretched hands and bobbing heads at the foot of the stage. Tonight, however, Springsteen was nowhere to be seen. From his seat high above, the fan leaned over the railing and scanned the crowd intently, yet there was no sign of the wiry, dark-haired singer. This was very unusual. Had something happened to him? Had he fallen and been trampled by the crowd? Where was Springsteen?

Spotlights began to pan around the cavernous darkness of the Spectrum like searchlights signaling to a lost airplane on a foggy night. It seemed as if the people who were working the spotlights had also lost sight of Springsteen. The lights swept rapidly over the audience, both in the orchestra below and in the mezzanine seats far above.

Suddenly the spotlights stopped their scanning and focused on the first row of the mezzanine where the fan was sitting. He was temporarily blinded as the lights pointed directly at him. In the next instant the fan felt a

Bruce Springsteen performs amid a group of thrilled fans after one of his trademark jumps into the audience.

hand rest firmly on his shoulder. He peered over his shoulder to see who was bothering him. His heart almost came to a stop when he saw who it was. There, standing right next to him, was Bruce Springsteen.

Microphone in hand, Springsteen began to sing the last verse of "Spirit in the Night" as he stood in the mezzanine, 200 feet from the stage. Springsteen had not missed a note. Trailing hundreds of feet of microphone cable behind him and leading a small army of stage assistants and security staff, Springsteen had somehow managed to run through the hallways and stairs of the Spectrum to the mezzanine and emerge 45 seconds later, as if on cue, just as the saxophone solo ended.

The crowd erupted in cries of surprise and appreciation as it discovered the singer performing in the upper deck. In the mezzanine, the fan overcame his shock and reached out to shake the singer's hand. Within seconds, other fans began rushing toward Springsteen. In their exuberance, they threatened to trample him or, even worse, to knock him over the mezzanine railing and onto the crowd below. The security staff sprang into action, pushing back the crowd and rescuing the singer from his overeager fans. When the pushing and shoving ended, the fan found himself 20 feet from his seat.

Springsteen, now safely behind a small wall of security men, sang the song's closing lines with all his heart and soul, clearly as charged up as his audience. All 18,000 members of the crowd seemed to be singing with Springsteen during the final chorus, in which his calls of "Spirit in the night!" were met with a roar of voices responding, "All night!" The song reached its powerful conclusion, and the spotlights that had framed Springsteen as he sang suddenly went dark, covering his retreat from the mezzanine.

As Springsteen left the pandemonium upstairs and returned to the stage, the crowd, already on its feet, cheered, clapped, and stomped its appreciation. Cries of "Brooooooooce!" rang through the Spectrum. Springsteen and the E Street Band rocked and rolled for another three hours, before an audience that savored every sound and movement. Bruce Springsteen had returned to the stage, where he belonged, and the world of rock and roll was very glad to have him back.

2 "Growin' Up"

NEW JERSEY HAS LONG been a state with a bad reputation. Situated between New York and Pennsylvania, it is best known for its enormous network of ugly but functional highways, Atlantic City casinos, shopping malls, oil refineries, run-down seashore towns, and an endless sprawl of suburban communities. But New Jersey's reputation as an industrial wasteland is not entirely fair. Although it is true that some parts of the state suffer from poverty, pollution, crime, and other problems, New Jersey also has a considerable number of attractive and desirable areas. It boasts some of the most beautiful and exclusive suburbs in the nation, as well as, in Princeton, one of America's finest universities. A large portion of the southern part of the state is farmland, and the northern region contains scenic mountains and lakes that provide a vacation getaway for the entire Northeast.

New Jersey also has an unusually high number of suburban towns of varying levels of prosperity. Toward the lower end of the scale, in terms of wealth and beauty, is the town of Freehold. Fifteen miles inland from the Atlantic Ocean, Freehold is a small working-class town that has long been

Bruce Springsteen, shown here in his high school yearbook picture, was a loner who was far from popular with his classmates. He later recalled, "I hated high school! I had a terrible time in high school! When fall comes around, I'm *still* glad I don't have to go *back* to high school!"

economically dependent on a cluster of nearby factories. It was in the town of Freehold that Bruce Frederick Springsteen was born on September 23, 1949.

Bruce was the eldest of three children; his sisters, Virginia and Pamela, are 1 and 13 years younger, respectively. The family name is Dutch, although Springsteen and his sisters are mostly of Italian and Irish ancestry.

Springsteen's father, Douglas, held a number of jobs, working at various times as a factory worker, a bus driver, and a prison guard. But there were many periods of unemployment, and money was often in short supply. As a result, the Springsteens were forced to move fairly often, and occasionally they had to move in with relatives for brief periods.

Most American families of the time believed that through hard work and perseverance they could attain such goals as owning a house and buying a new car every few years. These simple symbols of success always seemed just beyond the reach of Douglas Springsteen. Bruce would later observe, "My father worked a lot of jobs that take everything from you and give nothing back."

Adele Springsteen, Bruce's mother, was the unifying force for the family during his childhood. Mrs. Springsteen worked as a legal secretary, and her income was important to the family's finances. Bruce later recalled "her refusal to be disheartened, even though she was really up against it a lot of the time. My mother lived with an immense amount of stress and pressure and she was a person of immense control. It was she who created the sense of stability in the family, so that we never felt threatened through all the hard times."

Unfortunately, Douglas Springsteen's employment failures sometimes strained his relationship with his family. From the time Bruce reached adolescence, he was often at odds with his father. There was little communication between the two. Both father and son were stubborn and had bad tempers when they were provoked. They argued frequently, until their arguments were almost their only contact.

Springsteen's troubled relationship with his father was a central issue in his life for many years. It would serve as the inspiration for several songs, as well as appear in some of the compelling real-life stories that he would sometimes use to introduce songs in concert. As he told the story one night,

> My father, he worked a lotta different places, worked in a rug mill for a while, drove a cab for a while, and he was a guard down at the jail for a while. I can remember when he worked down there, he used to always come home real pissed off, drunk, sit in the kitchen.
>
> At night, about nine o'clock, he used to shut off all the lights, every light in the house. And he used to get real pissed off if me or my sister turned any of 'em on. And he'd sit in the kitchen with a six pack and a cigarette. My mom, she'd set her hair and she would come downstairs and just turn on the TV and sit in the chair and watch TV till she fell asleep. And she'd get up the next morning and go to work again.
>
> My pop, sometimes he went to bed, sometimes he didn't. Sometimes he got up. Sometimes he didn't get up. And I used to sleep upstairs. In the summertime, when the weather got hot, I used to drag my mattress out the window and sleep on the roof next door to the gas station. And I watched these different guys—the station closed at one and these guys, they'd be pullin' in and pullin' out all night long. They'd be meetin' people there. They'd be rippin' off down the highway.
>
> As soon as I got sixteen, me and my buddy, we got this car and we started takin' off. We used to take off down to the beach, sleep on top of the beach houses. We used to spin up to the city, just walk around the streets all night long 'til the cops would catch us in the Port Authority and call our pops.

Still known today as the king of rock and roll, Elvis Presley, shown here in the 1950s, blended the rhythm and blues style of black musicians with a sped-up version of country and western music. His fans included the seven-year-old Bruce Springsteen, who upon seeing Presley for the first time on television turned to his mother and said, "I wanna be *just . . . like . . . that.*"

The Springsteens were Roman Catholics, and despite their financial hardships they found the money to send Bruce to St. Rose of Lima, a parochial school in the neighborhood. Whatever educational advantages the situation might have presented were lost on Bruce. According to Springsteen, "I was a big daydreamer when I was in grammar school. Kids used to tease me, call me a dreamer." Although he was bright, he was not a good student, and he did not get along with the strict nuns who were the teachers at the school.

As is often true in parochial schools, maintaining order was seemingly as important as educating a difficult student like Bruce. He hated the rigid discipline and authoritarian teaching methods of the nuns. Rather than trying harder to succeed at his studies, he stopped trying at all.

After completing the eighth grade, Bruce moved on to public high school, but his troubles continued. His rebelliousness increased, and he showed little interest in academics, athletics, and other school activities. Springsteen was a loner, with no close friends; he later said, "It was like I didn't exist." It was music that would provide Springsteen's escape from his empty life.

Like many other future musicians of his generation, Bruce Springsteen first became interested in music when he saw Elvis Presley on "The Ed Sullivan Show," the most popular television variety show at the time. Presley was tall and handsome, with long, black hair that was greased and swept back, and his exuberant body gyrations caused almost as much excitement as his vocals. Even at the age of seven, Bruce was captivated by the performance. He turned to his mother and said, "I wanna be *just . . . like . . . that.*"

Adele Springsteen shared some of her son's appreciation for Presley, and she encouraged Bruce when he expressed an interest in learning how to sing and play the guitar like his new idol. When Bruce was nine years old, his mother bought him a guitar. He was a little too young to master the instrument, and he soon grew bored with practicing. He put the guitar aside for a few years.

Rock and roll, though less than 10 years old, had grown stale and predictable in the years following the early triumphs of Elvis Presley, Chuck Berry, Little Richard, Jerry Lee Lewis, and other pioneers. In an attempt to broaden rock and roll's appeal, the music industry had promoted artists whose tame music and bland good looks made them less threatening than the rebellious early stars. By the early 1960s, rock and roll had become little different from the mainstream popular music it had seemed ready to overthrow.

In 1963, when Bruce was 13 years old, a quartet of young musicians from Liverpool, England, the Beatles, gave rock and roll a much needed burst of energy and inspiration. In February 1964, with their single "I Want To Hold Your Hand" racing to the top of the sales charts, the Beatles began a much heralded tour of the United States. They began with an appearance on "The Ed Sullivan Show," and their performance caused a tremendous sensation among young viewers, including Bruce Springsteen. The group was invited back to perform the following week, an unheard-of event in the 23-year history of the television program. Only a few weeks later, their songs held the top five positions on the singles charts, which was also an unprecedented feat.

In the wake of the Beatles' American triumph, a flood of other British groups, including the Rolling Stones, the

Kinks, the Who, the Animals, and the Dave Clark Five, released successful records in America. In what would soon be characterized as the British Invasion, these British bands virtually took over the American rock and roll scene within a year.

The simple charm of the British sound made it popular with young, aspiring musicians. A few inexpensive musical instruments, an amplifier or two, and a couple of microphones were all the equipment they needed. The young hopefuls had to learn only a few guitar chords or drum licks to play a song, and those who could put together a few chords and lyrics could write their own. Almost anyone, it seemed, could be in a band.

The Beatles, shown here during a 1966 television performance, dominated the popular music scene in the late 1960s. Within weeks of their arrival in America from England in 1963, their songs occupied the top five spots on the U.S. singles charts.

When he was 13, Bruce bought a guitar at a local pawnshop. For the first time, he knew what he wanted to do with his life: He wanted to play rock and roll. "Rock and roll, man, it changed my life," he later said. "It was liberating, the key out of the pits. Once I found the guitar I had the key to the highway!"

Much to the annoyance of his mother and, in particular, his father, Bruce Springsteen's commitment to rock and roll continued to grow. His father could not understand why Bruce was always playing "that goddamned guitar," as he called it. It was all Bruce seemed to care about. Sports held little appeal for him, and at this point he was too shy to show much interest in girls.

Bruce spent a lot of time listening to the radio. The rock and roll stations played not only the latest British sounds but also many exciting forms of American music. Springsteen's favorites included the soul music of Sam Cooke, Jackie Wilson, and Sam and Dave; Phil Spector's multilayered "wall of sound" productions; folk-rock performers such as the Byrds and Bob Dylan; the melodramatic teen dramas of Roy Orbison; and the raunchy rock and roll of Mitch Ryder and the Detroit Wheels.

As soon as he had taught himself the basics of playing the guitar, Springsteen joined a band called the Rogues. He was 14 years old and still in high school. The Rogues played occasional weekend dances at local schools, the Elks Club, and other places popular with teenagers in the Freehold area. Springsteen played guitar but sang no lead vocals, as the band featured another singer.

The Rogues broke up after about a year. A friend of Springsteen's, George Theiss, was the rhythm guitarist and lead singer for a local band called the Castiles. It was early in 1965, and the Castiles had just fired their lead guitarist. Theiss invited Springsteen to audition for the band, and Bruce leaped at the opportunity.

Tex Vinyard, a middle-aged factory worker, served as the Castiles' manager and allowed the band to rehearse in his home. Vinyard thought that Bruce was a nice kid, and it was obvious that the young guitarist was eager to impress both the manager and the band. In Vinyard's opinion, however, Springsteen was simply not ready to join the Castiles. He could play a little, but he did not know how to play any complete songs. Vinyard told Bruce to come back when he had learned four or five songs.

The very next night Springsteen returned to Vinyard's house and asked for another chance to play for him. Bruce had managed to teach himself the lead guitar parts of more than five songs in just one night, listening to the radio and then painstakingly repeating what he had heard. Vinyard remembered, "Well, this damn kid sat down and knocked out five songs that would blow your *ears.*"

Vinyard brought Springsteen to the Castiles' next rehearsal. As Tex described it,

> Bruce is standing there with his ass out of his jeans, his damn boots all run over, always in a T-shirt, pimples all over his face. So George says, "Bruce, why don't you show us what you learned?" . . . Well, Bruce cut loose with those damn things, and you shoulda seen the look on George's face. The drummer dropped his sticks. Bruce is real cool. He says, "How did I do? All right?" He's serious!
>
> Well, George just turned around to me and said, "Hey, Tex, I'm still lead singer, ain't I?" Bruce says, "Well, am I gonna make it in the band?" I said, "Son, as far as I'm concerned, you're in the band."

It was Vinyard's devotion to the band members that set them apart from thousands of similar groups across the country. Most of these bands never played anywhere other than in someone's basement or garage, and most broke up almost immediately. Few groups at the outset of their careers were lucky enough to have a manager who worked as selflessly and tirelessly as Vinyard. He did so knowing that he would never earn back the money he spent on the group. Vinyard liked the boys, and he loved rock and roll, so the Castiles' dream of becoming a rock and roll band was his dream, too.

Although he had never managed a band before, Vinyard proved to be so capable that soon other groups asked him to represent them as well. Eventually he became involved in the careers of 21 bands in the Freehold area. He managed all these groups while working a full-time factory job.

Vinyard and his wife, Marion, treated the Castiles as if they were their own sons. The five musicians were always welcome at the Vinyard home, even on days when no rehearsals were scheduled. The couple hosted the group's daily rehearsals and bought them badly needed musical equipment, even if such purchases meant that they would sacrifice their own comfort and needs. Springsteen was particularly fond of the Vinyards and even took to calling them Ma and Pa.

After six weeks of regular rehearsals, the Castiles were ready to play their first engagement. Vinyard got them a gig at a dance at a nearby swim club. He went deep into debt to buy the band some microphones and a big amplifier for the guitars. Though he was on strike at the time and taking in only $21 a week in union benefits, the boys begged him for a beautiful new $300 amplifier. "Might as well have been three thousand as far as I was concerned. But they had to have it, they just had to have it," he said. So, "I went into hock for it. I think I gave him 5 dollars down for it and it was 11 bucks a month—for about three years."

Armed with their new equipment, the Castiles were a big hit. The band collected their first professional fee of $35, from which they proudly gave Vinyard his 10-percent manager's fee—which came to all of $3.50.

Soon the Castiles were playing regularly at school dances and at no-alcohol teen clubs in Freehold. Once they even played at the local asylum. "This guy in a suit got up and introduced us for twenty minutes," Bruce later claimed. "Then the doctors came up and took him away." They performed every couple of weeks and developed a following among local teens. Springsteen was still something of a loner, and he suffered from a bad case of acne, but he enjoyed the attention he received as a member of the Castiles. George Theiss, the lead singer, received most of the attention from female fans, but for the first time, girls began to notice the shy Springsteen also, who now wore his hair in a shaggy, Beatles-style cut.

In May 1966, Vinyard paid for the band to go into a local recording studio to record a single, and the group performed two songs co-written by Bruce Springsteen and George Theiss. They composed the songs in the backseat of Tex's car on the way to the studio. The record was never released, but it gave Bruce and the other members of the band their first exposure to a recording studio. Springsteen also discovered that he enjoyed songwriting, and he began to turn out his own tunes, many of which ended up in the Castiles' play list.

From 1965 until his graduation from high school in 1967, Bruce Springsteen (far right), played lead guitar for the Castiles, a band composed mostly of high school students that was managed by factory worker Tex Vinyard. The Castiles achieved some success but the musicians went their separate ways after high school.

The Castiles' popularity continued to grow, and they began to get gigs at clubs near the Jersey Shore, 15 or 20 miles away from Freehold. By now the band had become polished and exciting, and it had developed a reputation as a terrific live act. Despite seemingly overwhelming competition from more experienced groups, the band auditioned for the opportunity to play a regular gig at Cafe Wha?, a club in New York City's Greenwich Village. Much to their surprise, they got the job. Their performances at Cafe Wha? were so well received that the Castiles were soon playing at clubs in the Village regularly, despite the inconvenience of the 90-minute trip from Freehold to Manhattan.

The enthusiastic audiences in New York occasionally included talent scouts for the many record companies located in the metropolis. Vinyard and the band had brief discussions with several companies, but none offered a recording contract. It was now 1967, and the music scene had started to change. The Castiles' look and sound had grown a little dated. Rock and roll was turning in new directions, and the Castiles' infectious but lightweight music was no longer in style.

In June 1967, Springsteen and most of the other members of the band graduated from high school. Being in a working rock and roll band had been enjoyable for all the group's members, but most of them decided that it was time to move on with their lives—to attend college, to get a regular job, or to get married. Only Bruce Springsteen remained committed to a career in music. As summer arrived, the Castiles went their separate ways.

3 "Backstreets"

AFTER THE CASTILES DISBANDED, Bruce Springsteen was on his own. He performed occasionally in the nearby town of Red Bank, at a small club that was owned by a friend. Playing his own songs and accompanying himself on acoustic guitar, Springsteen gained valuable experience in singing and entertaining an audience on his own. While he pondered the next move in his musical career, Springsteen began spending time in the music clubs and bars of Asbury Park.

Asbury Park is the largest town on the Jersey Shore north of Atlantic City. At the beginning of the 20th century, Asbury Park was a prosperous and popular summer resort where well-to-do city dwellers would come for the summer. In the era before air-conditioning, Asbury Park's sea breezes provided a much needed escape from the summer's heat. Visitors stayed at big, airy hotels or smaller guest houses, strolled along the mile-long boardwalk, and swam in the cooling Atlantic Ocean surf.

By 1968, however, Asbury Park had fallen on hard times. The city's downtown area, a half mile inland from the beach, became all but deserted.

Asbury Park, New Jersey, shown here in the early 20th century, was once a prosperous and popular summer resort town. Today it is best known for nurturing the early career and musical education of New Jersey native Bruce Springsteen.

29

By the time Bruce Springsteen began frequenting its bars and nightclubs in the 1970s, Asbury Park was no longer the genteel and luxurious town it had once been. Already run-down and ravaged by economic decline, on July 6, 1970, Asbury Park was the site of race riots, leaving such devastated businesses as this one on Springwood Avenue.

Poverty and unemployment increased. The situation grew even worse in 1970, when a series of violent race riots broke out. Much of what remained of the downtown area was damaged or destroyed, and the disturbances further discouraged visitors from coming to Asbury Park's beach area.

Asbury Park's famous boardwalk had survived through the years. Its early 20th-century elegance, however, had long since been replaced by third-rate amusement parks, pinball arcades, miniature golf courses, fortune-tellers, and other seedy attractions. The large crowds had stopped coming, and most who still visited came only for the day. Many hotels and other businesses that relied on tourism were forced to close.

A number of bars by the boardwalk managed to survive. Although most of the clubs featured bands that played the Top 40 hits of the day, it was also possible to hear rock and roll, psychedelic rock, blues, soul, and rhythm and blues. It was a great place for musicians to meet each other, to strike up new friendships, and to form new professional alliances.

Springsteen found the time he spent in the Asbury Park nightspots to be quite valuable. His musical interests began to change as he absorbed the new types of music he was exposed to. It was not long before he had formed a new band called Earth, a blues-rock trio featuring Bruce on electric guitar and vocals, along with an electric bass and drums.

Earth stayed together for about a year, playing in bars and clubs around the Jersey Shore. The band members worked fairly regularly but did not develop a large

following and never made very much money. They performed both Springsteen's compositions and covers of
popular songs. Springsteen's extended guitar solos, mod-
eled after those of Eric Clapton of Cream, were the
group's most obvious feature. He developed a reputation
as the fastest, if not the best, guitarist on the Asbury Park
scene, and other musicians began to notice his talents.

But music was not the only thing on the minds of
young people at the time. In the late 1960s, the specter
of the Vietnam War hung over the heads of every male
of draft age who was not able to escape to college. Most
young Americans were touched by the Vietnam War in
some way, even if they were not in the military themselves. Most had a friend, husband, cousin, neighbor, or
brother who served in Vietnam. Given the high number
of American casualties, many also knew someone who
had been killed or wounded in the war. For Bruce Springsteen, his most personal connection to the Vietnam War
was the battlefield death of Bart Haines, the Castiles'
drummer.

Although Springsteen was not interested in politics at
this point in his life, he had no wish to meet the same fate
that Haines and other young men had suffered in Vietnam. "You didn't want to go because you'd seen other
people go and not come back. We just knew we didn't
want to go and die."

When he was contacted by his local draft board offi-
cials, Springsteen convinced them that he was unfit for
the military. With his shoulder-length hair, ragged cloth-
ing, and rebellious nature, Springsteen appeared psycho-
logically unsuited for army life. Injuries to his leg and
head suffered in a recent motorcycle accident also dis-
qualified him from military service.

While his personality and appearance may have helped
keep Springsteen out of the armed forces, he looked more
like a rebel than he actually was. Unlike many people his

age, Springsteen never experimented with drugs of any kind. "When I was at the age when it was popular," he said, "I wasn't really in a social scene a whole lot. I was practicing in my room with my guitar. Plus, I was very concerned with being in control at the time." To this day, Springsteen says that he has never used drugs and that he drinks alcohol only occasionally and always in moderation.

Aside from music, the 18-year-old Springsteen had no hobbies or outside interests. Looking back, Springsteen seemed to regard this solitary life as the price one had to pay to become a musician. "I was working on the inside all the time," he said. "A lot of rock and roll people went through this solitary existence. If you're gonna be good at something, you've gotta be alone a lot to practice."

Springsteen enrolled at Ocean County Community College in 1968, motivated mostly by a desire to receive a student deferment from the military draft. He found college no more stimulating academically than high school had been. As in previous years of schooling, he did not find any teachers who could motivate and inspire him. His long hair and relatively grubby style of dress alienated the faculty and fellow students, some of whom actually sought his expulsion from the school. Springsteen dropped out of college after about a year.

He continued to live at home with his family until his father decided to make a fresh start, far from New Jersey. Douglas Springsteen moved his family to San Mateo, California, a small city south of San Francisco. Bruce decided to stay in New Jersey to pursue his budding musical career. He remained, illegally, in the rented house that his family had vacated, then moved into the first of several apartments that he shared briefly with fellow musicians.

By the time Earth broke up in early 1969, Springsteen was spending his free nights and postgig early morning

hours at the Upstage in Asbury Park. The Upstage had opened in 1968, two flights above a Thom McAn shoe store. It started as a private, after-hours club for musicians only but later opened its doors to the public. It was at the Upstage that Springsteen met two young musicians who were to become his close friends. John Lyon, alias Southside Johnny, was a singer and blues harmonica player and a rhythm and blues fanatic. The other, Miami Steve Van Zandt, was a talented guitarist. The three men were among the most promising musicians who spent time at the Upstage, and they would be at the heart of the Asbury Park music scene for many years.

In the notes he wrote for the back cover of Southside Johnny's first album in 1976, Bruce Springsteen described the scene at the Upstage. "There were a lotta musicians there, 'cause the bands that came down from North Jersey to play in the Top 40 clubs along the shore

A crowd of thousands jams the boardwalk of Asbury Park on May 31, 1970. The Asbury Park of Bruce Springsteen's early career was a seedy carnival of pinball arcades, fortune-tellers, and amusement parks. Springsteen sometimes slept on the beach after playing all night in Asbury Park's nightclubs.

would usually end up there after their regular gig, along with a lot of different guys from the local areas. Everybody went there 'cause it was open later than the regular clubs and because between one and five in the morning you could play pretty much whatever you wanted, and if you were good enough, you could choose the guys you wanted to play with."

Southside Johnny said of the Upstage, "It was a good learning place. People would come from all over to play there, people you never saw before. You'd meet musicians there, you'd hear new things. There were some terrible musicians, terrible bands, but occasionally there was someone who really inspired you."

The music played all evening and well into the morning hours, as musicians took the stage in various combinations. Sometimes they were asked to play in the house band that performed throughout the night, and the club's management slipped the musicians $10 apiece for their efforts; most were only too glad to receive the money. One never knew who one would be playing with on any particular evening or what type of music would be played, so the musicians had to be quick learners and good listeners.

Bruce Springsteen soon gained a reputation as the most talented musician who frequented the Upstage. Older, more experienced musicians grew to appreciate his abilities and were eager to play with him. When Springsteen was ready to form a new group after the breakup of Earth, there was no shortage of Upstage regulars who were willing to work with him. He auditioned many musicians before finally settling on the band's lineup.

Springsteen's new band was at first called Child, but when it turned out that another band was using that name, the band settled on the name Steel Mill. In addition to Springsteen on guitar and lead vocals, the group featured organist Danny Federici, drummer Vini Lopez, and bass guitarist Vinny Roslyn. Roslyn was later fired by Springsteen and replaced by Steve Van Zandt. Van Zandt was really a guitarist, but because Springsteen wanted him in the band he learned how to play the bass guitar.

Most of the songs performed by Steel Mill were written by Springsteen. Because they played mostly original material, Steel Mill found it difficult to get gigs at Asbury Park's largest clubs, which preferred groups who played Top 40 hits. The band, however, found engagements at smaller clubs and bars in the Jersey Shore area, and it continued to play regularly at the Upstage. Although Springsteen was the leader of Steel Mill, the group split its fees equally among the members.

Steel Mill needed a place to rehearse, and they found one through their manager, Tinker West. West, who was from California, owned and managed a small surfboard factory. He agreed to allow the band to use the factory building as a rehearsal hall. When Springsteen, Van Zandt, and Lopez needed a place to live, West offered to let them live there as well. The three musicians occasionally worked around the factory to pay for their rent. This work was as close to holding a regular, nonmusical job as Springsteen would ever come in his life. As a result of his exposure to surfboards and surfers around the factory, Springsteen actually began surfing, and he became good at the sport.

Tinker West and Springsteen became close friends. It was West who finally taught Springsteen

A crowd gathers outside the Stone Pony, one of the legendary clubs in Asbury Park where Bruce Springsteen often played in the 1970s.

how to drive. Springsteen did not learn how to drive a car until he was 19 years old, which is extremely late for a young man growing up in the wide open spaces of New Jersey. This seems especially ironic given the importance of automobiles in many of his songs. It may also explain why he spent so much time practicing the guitar at home.

West proved to be a capable manager, and Steel Mill worked regularly at bars and clubs throughout central New Jersey. West also got the band engagements in college towns in New Jersey and elsewhere on the East Coast. Steel Mill developed an enthusiastic following in Richmond, Virginia, where the band soon began performing frequently.

In 1969, Tinker West decided to visit his parents in California, and he offered to take Springsteen and the band along. Springsteen visited his family in San Mateo. Steel Mill played a few gigs at clubs in the San Francisco Bay Area, but there was little enthusiasm for the New Jersey band in California. Steel Mill returned to the familiar, more appreciative circuit of Asbury Park, the Jersey Shore, and Richmond.

When Steel Mill went back to the Bay Area a year later, the band's performance received a much warmer reception. West arranged for Steel Mill to play at the Matrix in Berkeley, which was one of the area's most popular rock clubs. One show was reviewed in the *San Francisco Examiner,* a major daily newspaper. The reviewer, Philip Elwood, raved about the band, calling the performance "one of the most memorable evenings of rock in a long time by totally unknown talent." Elwood also wrote, "I have never been so overwhelmed by an unknown band." Springsteen's songs, in particular, drew high praise from the critic. It marked the first time that Springsteen's music had been reviewed in a major publication, and the praise could not have been more enthusiastic.

One person who read the *Examiner* review was rock impresario Bill Graham. Graham, the best-known concert promoter in the country, ran rock's most prestigious concert halls, the Fillmore West in San Francisco and the Fillmore East in New York City, and also had a small record company. On the strength of the review in the *Examiner,* Graham invited Steel Mill to perform at a Fillmore West audition night.

The band impressed Graham enough that he invited them into the recording studio to make some demo recordings, which are essentially a recorded audition, and offered them a contract with his record company. But the money he was willing to advance to the band was only about $1,000, a meager amount even to a struggling band like Steel Mill. On Tinker West's advice, they rejected the offer. Heartened by their success at the Matrix, but disappointed that it had not led to a better contract offer, Steel Mill drove back to New Jersey.

Springsteen's enthusiasm for Steel Mill had begun to wane even before the band returned from San Francisco. The band was performing regularly and was getting good reviews from New Jersey newspapers. For all their efforts, however, the group was making relatively little money. It was frustrating for Springsteen and his fellow musicians to return to the routine of playing the same smoky bars and clubs, and it was becoming increasingly obvious that Steel Mill was not likely to become a major success.

Wishing to concentrate on his guitar playing rather than his singing, Springsteen had the group hire a singer to handle the lead vocals. Even surrendering his vocal responsibilities could not reawaken Springsteen's diminishing interest in the band. He had grown bored with the band's hard rock sound and the limitations of the four-piece instrumentation, and he was eager to explore new directions in his music. Early in 1971, after almost three years together, Springsteen disbanded Steel Mill.

4 "Thundercrack"

AFTER THE BREAKUP OF STEEL MILL, Bruce Springsteen set to work forming a new band. He envisioned a group substantially larger than his old band's four-man configuration, which would include horn players and female backup singers.

From Steel Mill, Springsteen kept Vini Lopez on drums and Steve Van Zandt, now back on guitar, for the new band. He added bassist Garry Tallent and keyboard player David Sancious, both veterans of other Asbury Park groups. Springsteen also advertised for additional musicians in a local newspaper. He spent months auditioning musicians and rehearsing his band before they were ready for their first engagement. The band's music had a strong rhythm and blues influence and was a major departure from the musical style of Steel Mill. Because the group was clearly the product of its leader's ideas and vision, it made sense that it was called the Bruce Springsteen Band.

For a variety of reasons, the Bruce Springsteen Band did not perform in public for six months after its formation in early 1971. It took time to work

The small clubs of New York City's Greenwich Village launched the careers of many of rock and roll's greatest stars. The Cafe Wha?, shown here in 1966, gave Bruce Springsteen his first big break in New York when he was still performing with the Castiles.

the horn players and backup singers into the musical mixture. Also, Springsteen was writing a number of strong new songs to utilize his band's capabilities, and as a result, the band was constantly learning songs. Making matters more difficult was that, because of the race riots of the previous summer, the Asbury Park music scene was in a period of decline. Fewer patrons than ever came to the town, and many clubs and bars closed or discontinued live music. Consequently, when the Bruce Springsteen Band was ready to perform, there were few opportunities available. With 10 members, the group's unusually large size did not make it easy to find work, as few clubs could accommodate so many musicians. Furthermore, any fees the band earned would have to be split 10 ways, which was almost a guarantee that the band's members would earn very little money.

Almost as a joke, and to relieve the frustrations he and his fellow musicians were experiencing, Springsteen decided to put together a second band, the infamous Dr. Zoom and the Sonic Boom. Southside Johnny recalled the moment that Springsteen conceived Dr. Zoom, saying, "Let's put together a band of everybody who doesn't have any money and play a few dates."

On any given night, Dr. Zoom and the Sonic Boom consisted of as many as 30 members, including musicians, singers, baton twirlers, and almost anybody else who wished to belong. It was a crazy and colorful circus, an onstage party, and those in the band enjoyed the show at least as much as those in the audience. "Somebody'd take a solo and we'd all fall down laughing," Springsteen remembered. Those who wanted to join Dr. Zoom but were not able to play an instrument or sing could join the Monopoly game that took place onstage during the show—"You know, so they could say, 'Yeah, I'm in Dr. Zoom. I play Monopoly,'" Springsteen recalled years later.

The band played only three performances, but one came as the opening act for the Allman Brothers Band, a southern rock group that had recently become a national sensation. None of the band members made more than a few dollars for their efforts, but it was a tremendous morale booster for Springsteen and the rest of the Asbury Park music scene at a time when making a living in music had ceased to be much fun.

The Bruce Springsteen Band finally rounded into shape and was ready to begin performing. It was not easy to get a gig, but the band was eventually booked in Richmond, Virginia. The shows did not go very well for various reasons, not the least of which was the band's unwieldy size. When the band returned to New Jersey, the horn players and female vocalists were dismissed.

The Bruce Springsteen Band began to work the Jersey Shore music circuit as a five-piece band. On one rainy and windswept night the group played to a virtually empty club. As the band had agreed to play for the one dollar cover charge that was collected from each patron, they already knew that they would make very little money. Springsteen and Van Zandt had gone out to the deserted street between sets and were returning to the club for the night's last performance. Out of the mist an enormous man who neither Springsteen nor Van Zandt had ever seen before approached the two musicians. He was dressed entirely in white and was carrying a saxophone. According to a story that would be acted out theatrically in dozens of future concerts, the two men cowered in fear until the stranger finally introduced himself.

Saxophonist Clarence Clemons, a former college football player and a veteran of rhythm and blues bands in Virginia, Maryland, and New Jersey, had heard terrific things about Springsteen and his band and had come after his own gig to sit in with Springsteen's band during its last set. There was an almost instant musical bond between Clemons and Springsteen. Clemons recalled later, "We looked at each other that day and we knew—right then—where it was at. It was like we had been playing together for years. All the things I'd been searching for, all the bands I'd played in, everything was right there—and it blew me away." Almost immediately Clarence Clemons became a permanent member of the Bruce Springsteen band.

The band of Springsteen, Van Zandt on guitar, keyboardist David Sancious, Garry Tallent on bass, Vini Lopez on drums, and now Clarence Clemons became very close friends. They stuck together through months of struggling, with few gigs and very little money. Springsteen would later describe splitting hot dogs four ways among his friends when they were broke. Nobody quit, though; it was as if they all sensed it was only a matter of time until Springsteen became a success. Springsteen was just as loyal to his band members, to the extent of splitting all fees they earned equally among them, despite Springsteen's dominant role in the group.

The slump in the Asbury Park music scene dragged on, however, and Springsteen began to take occasional solo engagements in New York City to earn some money. By late 1971 he needed to take a break from the Asbury Park scene, partially as a result of the lack of work and apparently also because of some complications in his love life.

Although Springsteen has always been protective of his private life and seldom discusses it publicly, it has been said that from early adulthood on he was rarely without a girlfriend. The awkward teenager had grown into a handsome man whose dark curly hair, rugged features, and wiry physique many women found attractive. Certainly his charisma as a performer also contributed to his appeal. But music was Springsteen's first love, and his career always came before his love life.

To escape from Asbury Park, Springsteen returned to California by himself, this time for an extended stay. He even considered moving to California permanently. Springsteen lived with his family in San Mateo for a while, and apparently they got along well. The tensions between Douglas Springsteen and his son had been reduced by the passage of time and the family's relocation. The whole family even took a brief trip down to Mexico.

Springsteen also tested the music scene in the Bay Area, but he had difficulty finding musicians with whom to play. Most of those he met were high school boys who were still practicing in their parents' garages. The Jersey Shore scene began to seem a lot more attractive to the 22-year-old. By February 1972 he was back in Asbury Park.

With their leader on the West Coast and perhaps intending to stay there, the Bruce Springsteen Band had

Bruce Springsteen relaxes in a quiet, sawdust-littered cafe in 1971. When he first signed with Columbia Records, the company envisioned Springsteen as a solo singer-songwriter along the lines of Bob Dylan, who came out of the folk music movement of the 1960s.

continued to play occasional gigs, with Steve Van Zandt assuming temporary command. But they were all forced to turn to jobs outside performing to make ends meet. Clarence Clemons, for example, worked with children as a social worker. Van Zandt worked at construction jobs until he took a job as the bandleader for the Dovells, an oldies act that was still performing regularly on the strength of two hits it had had more than a decade earlier. Garry Tallent gave guitar lessons to children.

When Springsteen returned to New Jersey, he chose not to reconvene his band, at least not right away. He had another strategy in mind. Putting his years of playing in rock bands behind him, at least temporarily, he decided to sell himself as a solo act. As a center of the music industry, New York was the obvious place to turn. Tinker West, Steel Mill's manager and Springsteen's close friend, had met a pair of songwriters and record producers, Mike Appel and Jim Cretecos, who were looking for singer-songwriters to manage and produce. Their main claim to fame was that they had written a hit song for the Partridge Family, "Doesn't Somebody Want To Be Wanted."

Bruce Springsteen had met Appel and Cretecos before he left for California, at a meeting arranged by Tinker West in November 1971. The two were only mildly impressed with Springsteen, who auditioned for them in their Manhattan office. Appel remembered the meeting: "He was wearing ripped-up jeans and a T-shirt. He said he wanted to get an album deal with a major label. I remember he looked at me and said, 'I'm tired of being a big fish in a little pond.' 'Fine,' I said, 'let's hear what you've got.' So he sat down at the piano and played only two songs. The first was the most boring thing I'd ever heard in my entire life. But the second had something. It was a song about dancing with a girl who was deaf, dumb, and blind with a lyric that included, 'They danced all night to a silent band.' It was a very weird line and it stuck in my head, as did the way he sang, with an intensity I couldn't believe. He sang like his life depended on it. Still, I didn't feel the earth move beneath me."

They were not sufficiently impressed with Springsteen's abilities at the time to sign the young singer to a management contract. Instead Appel advised Springsteen to write some more songs and to contact them again in the future. Three months later, when he had returned from California, Springsteen called Appel for an appointment. At first the manager did not remember him, until the singer mentioned their mutual connection through Tinker West. Later that day Springsteen drove up from New Jersey, and that evening he auditioned again for Appel and Cretecos.

This time there was no doubt. Springsteen played eight new songs, and Appel remembers being amazed by all of them, describing them as "the most poetic, potent and powerful lyrics I've ever heard to this day." When Springsteen finished the last song, Appel said to him, "Look, all I can tell you is I want to go forward. I want to take your songs around to record companies." Appel convinced Springsteen that no one would work harder to get him a recording contract and build his career.

Within several weeks Springsteen signed the first of three contracts with Laurel Canyon Ltd., the new production company formed by Appel and Cretecos. Without having an attorney review the documents, which is the usual procedure, Springsteen signed a long-term management contract on the hood of a parked car in the parking lot of a bar. Ultimately, failing to consult with an attorney would prove to be the biggest mistake of Springsteen's career.

Appel's enthusiasm for Springsteen's music was genuine. An intense and aggressive man, Appel's strong personality was his most recognizable attribute, in both positive and negative ways. A former U.S. Marine, he could use his bullying nature to get his way in some situations, but his aggressiveness could often be so obnoxious that it would damage his own cause.

Despite his inexperience as a manager, Appel succeeded within weeks in getting Springsteen the big breakthrough he had been seeking. In a typically brash move he telephoned the office of Columbia Records talent scout John Hammond. Through sheer audacity and persistence, as well as some creative fibbing, Appel convinced Hammond's secretary to schedule a personal

Columbia Records' greatest talent scout, John Hammond (right), confers with two of the musical geniuses he discovered for Columbia: rock giant Bob Dylan (left) and jazz titan Benny Goodman (center). Hammond said that upon hearing Bruce Springsteen for the first time, "I knew at once that he would last a generation."

audition for the unknown manager and the obscure young singer. This was a major accomplishment.

John Hammond was one of the true legends of the music industry. Born in 1910 into a branch of one of America's wealthiest families, his career had already spanned more than 40 years on the day he met Bruce Springsteen in June 1972. Hammond had discovered some of the greatest performers in American music, including Billie Holiday, Count Basie, Bob Dylan, and Aretha Franklin. Hammond had signed all these talents

to Columbia Records, the largest and most well-known record company in the world.

Springsteen had recently read a biography of Bob Dylan and from it had learned how John Hammond had discovered the unpolished young folksinger and signed him to Columbia Records in 1961. When other executives at Columbia heard Dylan, many thought that Hammond had finally lost his abilities as a judge of talent. Some called Dylan "Hammond's Folly," predicting that the talent scout's days at Columbia Records would soon come to an end. But Hammond stuck by his evaluation, staking his own reputation on Dylan's potential. Within a few years Dylan developed into one of the most accomplished and influential songwriters in the history of American music. If Hammond could recognize and nurture a talent as rough as the young Dylan, he might be able to do the same for Springsteen.

When Hammond checked his appointment calendar and saw the name Mike Appel, he had no idea who he was meeting or why, as the manager had lied his way onto the talent scout's crowded schedule. Hammond decided to keep the appointment anyway, but as soon as he met Appel he wished he had not. Appel sat down and said, "So you're the guy who was supposed to have found Bob Dylan. I wanna see if you've got ears, because I've got somebody much better than him."

"For God's sake, just stop it!" replied the shocked Hammond. "You're gonna make me hate you." Hammond said later that he considered Appel "about as offensive as any man I've ever met."

Appalled by Appel's rude behavior, Hammond turned his attention instead to Springsteen. Unlike his manager, Springsteen was thrilled just to be there. "I was broke, I didn't have any dough, I had nothin' goin', it was just the biggest thrill of my life, the day I came to his office." He, too, was horrified by Appel's conduct. "I'm shrivelin' up and I'm thinkin', 'Please, Mike, give me a break. Let me play a damn song.'"

The first song the singer performed was "It's Hard To Be a Saint in the City," a tune that would appear on Springsteen's first album. Hammond immediately knew that he was experiencing something very special. "Bruce was sort of grinning through this whole thing," Hammond remembered. "And I was just absolutely knocked out. . . . I've heard so many hundreds of people, and he's the first guy who's ever come through to me this way, much more than Dylan. I couldn't believe it. I knew at once that he would last a generation."

A live performance at the Gaslight, a Greenwich Village club, was quickly arranged for that evening, as Hammond also wanted to hear Springsteen perform before an audience. Accompanying himself on guitar, Springsteen captivated a small audience that included Hammond and some associates from Columbia Records. The next day Hammond and Springsteen went into a studio and recorded demo versions of his best songs. By now John Hammond was completely won over. Bruce Springsteen was soon recording his first album for Columbia.

5 "Thunder Road"

TECHNICALLY BRUCE SPRINGSTEEN WAS NOT SIGNED as a recording artist to Columbia Records. Among the three contracts he had signed with Mike Appel and Jim Cretecos's Laurel Canyon Ltd. was a recording deal that bound him to record for the production company. Laurel Canyon then made a deal with Columbia Records for the release of Springsteen's recordings. As a result Columbia had no direct agreement with Springsteen. All negotiations and communications had to be directed through Laurel Canyon, which was both a complication and an inconvenience for the record company.

Although he did not yet realize it, there were disadvantages from Springsteen's point of view as well. All monetary advances under the contract with Columbia were payable to Laurel Canyon, not to Springsteen. Any sums that would be earned through record sales were deliverable, once again, to Laurel Canyon. This situation placed Springsteen in the position of having no direct access to his own earnings. An independent attorney characterized the agreement as "a slavery deal."

After he was discovered by talent scout John Hammond in 1972, Columbia Records made a failed attempt to promote Springsteen as "the next Dylan." It would take years of struggle and false starts before Springsteen, shown here in 1975, would break through to true mass stardom.

If no major disagreements developed between Springsteen and Laurel Canyon, this situation would be more of an inconvenience than a serious problem. If, however, there were any conflicts between Springsteen and Laurel Canyon, Springsteen could be denied access to his own income. The management contract also granted Laurel Canyon 50 percent of the net profits, an absurdly large percentage. (The percentage was reportedly adjusted to a still excessive 20 percent at a later date.) Although there was nothing illegal about this situation, it was certainly not a fair one for Springsteen.

John Hammond learned of this arrangement before the deal between Laurel Canyon and Columbia was signed, and he was very concerned. Hammond felt that Appel was taking advantage of Springsteen's innocence as well as his inexperience in the music industry. Springsteen himself later said, "I never knew anyone who made a record or was involved in the record business. If they'd told me that part of the deal was mopping the floor, I suppose I'd have mopped the floor."

It was Hammond's opinion that the arrangement between Springsteen and Laurel Canyon would cause major problems at a later date. He expressed these beliefs to both Appel and Springsteen. Appel, however, would not revise the original agreement despite Hammond's warning. Springsteen was very loyal to Appel, whom he considered to be his friend as well as his manager, and would not even consider the possibility that Appel was not acting in his best interest. Having expressed his concerns to both sides and having been ignored, Hammond refused to interfere any further in the relationship between Springsteen and Appel.

Laurel Canyon received $65,000 from Columbia, of which $25,000 was an advance against future profits from the sale of Springsteen's recordings, a moderately large amount of money for an unknown and unproven performer. Springsteen's portion of the advance was by far the largest sum of money he had earned in his career. The remaining $40,000 was to be used for recording the first album.

While $40,000 may have seemed like a lot of money, even in 1972 it was not a large sum with which to make a record, because recording is very costly. It is easy to spend a fortune on studio time, particularly if the artist records at a first-rate, state-of-the-art facility. Recording studios charge by the hour for use of the studio and equipment. The major studios in New York City, which were the most convenient ones for Springsteen to use, were very expensive.

Mike Appel wanted to ensure that the $40,000 would be sufficient to pay for Springsteen's recording sessions. He also knew that any money that was left over would be retained by Laurel Canyon. With this in mind Appel arranged for Springsteen to record at tiny 914 Sound Studios in Blauvelt, New York, about 30 miles north of midtown Manhattan. The studio charged less than half the hourly rate of the major New York City studios. Located in a drab brick building a few yards off Route 303, 914 Sound Studios looked more like a plumbing supply business than a recording studio. Inside, the situation was no more impressive. The recording equipment was not top quality and was subject to mechanical problems, and the studio's acoustics were also not the best.

The technical qualities of a studio can have a major effect on the quality of a recording as well as on its commercial success. If a recording is poorly made, it is usually apparent to the listener, and many good songs and performances have been buried beneath an inferior production. Appel's decision to record at 914 Sound Studios to save money was risky and shortsighted. But Appel defended his choice, claiming that 914 Sound Studios was a "top-notch facility" and that "there was

Bruce Springsteen (center) mugs with the members of his band. From left to right are drummer Vini Lopez and organist Danny Federici, both holdovers from Steel Mill, bassist Garry Tallent, and saxophonist Clarence Clemons.

nothing we were doing that needed the excellence of a high-grade studio."

Before the recording sessions began, Springsteen informed both Mike Appel and Columbia Records that he wished to reassemble his band for use on the recordings. Both his manager and his record label were very surprised. They had only heard him perform solo, accompanying himself on acoustic guitar and, occasionally, piano and

had assumed that he would use the same format on his first record. Springsteen, however, had always intended to put together his old band when he got a recording deal, and on this point he was insistent. Clarence Clemons, Vini Lopez, Garry Tallent, and David Sancious were eager and ready to join Springsteen in the recording studio and in performances. Organist Danny Federici, a former member of Steel Mill, returned shortly after the

recording sessions were completed. Only Steve Van Zandt was absent, deciding to pursue other opportunities for the time being.

It was August 1972 when Springsteen entered the studio to record his first album. Just three weeks later the album was complete. In homage to his musical roots, Spring- steen decided to call the album *Greetings from As- bury Park, N.J.* The cover bore a reproduction of a classic postcard from As- bury Park's heyday as a beach resort.

The album consisted of nine songs, all of which were Springsteen originals and many of which had been featured at his audi- tions for Appel and Ham- mond earlier in the year. As expected, because of

the studio's deficiencies, the sound quality of the recording is flat and muffled. The band is featured on most of
the songs, but the overall sound of the album is gentle
and folkish, with the keyboards and saxophone parts
often having greater prominence than Springsteen's guitar. On many of the songs, Springsteen used an acoustic
rather than an electric guitar.

Springsteen's inexperience in the recording studio also
hampered him. Appel recalled that "Bruce had a lot of
ideas, but he wasn't knowledgeable about the studio. He
had definite ideas, so many that he didn't know which
one to pursue." Unfortunately, neither Appel nor Cretecos, who were listed as the album's producers and therefore had the responsibility of overseeing and directing the
recording process, could offer much guidance.

The songs suffer from occasional inconsistency in
terms of the quality and clarity of the lyrics, but the
album's release marked the emergence of a major songwriting talent. These songs, the earliest readily available
samples of Springsteen's abilities, reveal a playful and
exuberant tunesmith with an unusual capacity for creating striking and colorful images in his lyrics.

The album opens in a rush of energy with "Blinded
by the Light," an ebullient, guitar-driven song featuring
an explosion of word-game lyrics and poetic images.
"Growin' Up," a look back at Springsteen's own adoles-
cent years, puts a humorous twist on the emotional pain
and isolation he had actually experienced. "For You," a
bittersweet story of a failed relationship, is one of the
album's most intense songs, and as close to a love song as
any on the recording.

The album's centerpiece is "Spirit in the Night."
"Spirit"'s music has a jazzy, late-night feel that is the
perfect match for its inspired lyrics. The narrator and a
cast of characters with such colorful names as Crazy

Janey, Wild Billy, and Hazy Davy decide to drive to Greasy Lake for an all-night party at which passion, anger, and jealousy all burst forth beneath the moon and stars. Clarence Clemons's powerful tenor sax dances through the song in perfect contrast to Springsteen's impassioned vocals.

The recording sessions, budgeted by Columbia Records at $40,000, had cost only $11,000. The balance was kept by Laurel Canyon for its own use. Some money was spent on organizational expenses, and the remainder was used for the living expenses of Springsteen, his band, and his managers. Toward the end of 1972, Springsteen and the band played at clubs in Pennsylvania, Ohio, New York, and Massachusetts to generate income while they awaited the release of *Greetings*.

Although recording was completed by late summer, Columbia Records delayed releasing *Greetings from Asbury Park, N.J.* until after the Christmas holiday season, the busiest time of the year for record sales. The reason for the delay was that Columbia Records had little confidence in the commercial potential of Springsteen's record. There was little enthusiasm for the album among the executives at the record label.

The music on *Greetings* seemed to fall between categories, and record labels are notoriously incapable of marketing performers who are not easily categorized. For example, some of the musical arrangements on *Greetings* had a rock and roll or a rhythm and blues influence that was alien to the laid-back singer-songwriter audience. Conversely, the strong emphasis on the lyrics and the relatively low-key musical arrangements were not likely to attract the younger fans who followed heavy metal bands such as Led Zeppelin.

When *Greetings* was finally released in January 1973, it was accompanied by a publicity campaign that proved

This rare photograph of Bruce Springsteen was taken in 1972, the year he recorded *Greetings from Asbury Park, N.J.,* his first album. The record sold so poorly that there was some doubt as to whether Columbia Records would ask him to record another.

to be disastrous. The campaign for *Greetings* sought to capitalize on the connection with John Hammond and his reputation as the man who discovered Bob Dylan. In the advertisements and publicity materials that were sent to radio stations and record stores, Springsteen was called "The Next Dylan." It was a big mistake. Many people assumed that Springsteen was just another in a long line of inferior Dylan imitators. Rather than boost Springsteen's career, Columbia's overzealous publicity campaign provoked a terrible backlash. Many people hated Bruce Springsteen before they had ever heard his music. While most critics saw promise in his highly original if inconsistent songwriting, other reviewers focused on the excessive hype that surrounded Springsteen rather than considering his music.

Greetings from Asbury Park, N.J. was a commercial failure. It sold fewer than 12,000 copies in the first year of its release, a tiny number for an artist on a major label like Columbia. The two songs released as singles, "Blinded by the Light" and "Spirit in the Night," also sold poorly. On the basis of the response to *Greetings,* it was unclear whether Springsteen would receive the opportunity to record a second album for Columbia.

Bruce Springsteen and his band spent the early months of 1973 on a concert tour that took them mostly to college towns on the East Coast but also included a few dates in California. Springsteen played a number of gigs in the Philadelphia area at local colleges and clubs, where he was well received; one April performance was even broadcast later over a local radio station. Springsteen performed before enthusiastic audiences, but he was playing in such small clubs that the favorable response he received could hardly be expected to generate increased sales for his album.

Mike Appel decided that it was necessary to take a more aggressive approach in promoting the album. In conjunction with a new concert booking agent, Appel arranged for Springsteen and the band to perform as the opening act for Chicago, a rock group whose mellow pop hits had made them one of the most popular and successful bands in America. The idea was that Springsteen would be exposed every night to young audiences that might otherwise never hear his music. It seemed like an ideal method for increasing the size of his audience.

The tour consisted of concerts held in large sports arenas in nine cities. Springsteen and the band opened each concert by performing before an audience that had come to hear the popular band Chicago re-create its radio hits. The crowd had little interest in a new performer whom it had never heard. Springsteen's music was so different from Chicago's that it held little appeal for the audience anyway. No matter how hard Springsteen and his band worked onstage, they could not capture the crowd's attention. In many places they were actually booed by the impatient audience.

The most damaging performance of the brief tour was at New York's Madison Square Garden. Probably due to a lack of time, Springsteen and the band were denied a sound check (to optimize the band's sound prior to the start of the concert). As a result the sound quality was terrible. The band performed poorly before an audience that included many Columbia Records executives and staff members, whose confidence in their artist was shaken by the performance.

The Chicago tour was a demoralizing experience for Springsteen, and he vowed never again to be an opening act for a performer whose music was so different from his own. He refused to perform at sports arenas even as the headlining act for more than three years. Springsteen returned to the more comfortable club and college circuit of the Northeast for the rest of the year.

In July 1973, Springsteen and the band were invited to perform at a CBS Records convention, CBS being the parent company of Columbia Records. It was an opportunity to win over those at Columbia who had not been convinced of his abilities by the music on the album. The performance did not go well. Springsteen was uncharacteristically nervous when he went onstage, and it was evident in his performance. John Hammond was in the audience. "Bruce came on with a chip on his shoulder and played way too long," Hammond remembered. "People came to me and said, 'He can't really be that bad, can he, John?' Bruce came off sort of cocky. Remember, the album wasn't that big a seller, and the salespeople and promotion people, and other top-notch people, just hated it. Bruce was sort of patronizing the audience and afterward I said to him, 'Bruce, you blew it. What in God's name were you trying to do?'"

6 "The E Street Shuffle"

THE FIRST HALF OF 1973 had been a discouraging time for Bruce Springsteen. Aware that his future as a recording artist was very much in doubt, he returned to 914 Sound Studios with the band in July 1973 to record their second album. Because the recording budget was as limited as it had been for the first album, they recorded mostly in sessions held after midnight, when the studio's rates were lowest.

Mike Appel had to work hard to convince the executives at Columbia Records that Springsteen deserved the opportunity to record again. *Greetings from Asbury Park, N.J.* had sold so poorly that the record company's investment of $65,000 was considered nearly a total loss. Often in such situations a company will decide that it had made a mistake in signing the artist in the first place and will release the performer from the remainder of his or her contract. Many expected this fate for Springsteen.

Appel argued that there had been many encouraging reviews for *Greetings* and that, despite the twin fiascos of the Madison Square Garden concert and the performance at the CBS Records convention, Springsteen was building a

Springsteen's second album, *The Wild, the Innocent and the E Street Shuffle,* received almost no promotion from Columbia Records. But on the strength of more than 100 live performances in 1974, Springsteen's popularity grew and the album's sales quickly passed the 100,000 mark.

reputation as an exciting live performer. Knowing that its only hope of recouping the label's $65,000 outlay was to take a chance on the success of a second album, Columbia gave Appel another sizable monetary advance to cover the cost of recording another album.

The recording sessions lasted two months, and between their stints in the studio Springsteen and the band also performed at clubs and colleges several times a week. The leftover advance money from the first album was long gone, the advance for the second album was all earmarked to pay for studio time, and there was no further income from *Greetings,* as the album had not even covered its costs. Springsteen and his musicians, as well as their managers, were completely dependent on the income from live performances.

The new record was entitled *The Wild, the Innocent and the E Street Shuffle,* and it was released in November 1973, Springsteen's second album in 10 months. It featured a close-up photo of a bearded and intense Springsteen, seemingly lost deep in thought.

The album's first track, "The E Street Shuffle," is an upbeat and infectious rhythm-and-blues-flavored number that features a ragged horn section, dense percussion, spirited group vocals, and assorted party noises. The next song could not be more different from the first. "4th of July, Asbury Park (Sandy)" is a love song set on the beach and boardwalk of Asbury Park. Danny Federici's accordion, an old-fashioned instrument that is not often heard on rock albums, adds another romantic element to the song.

Two memorable songs perhaps best represented Springsteen's tremendous musical growth. "Incident on 57th Street" is a stunning and dramatic depiction of urban romance, played out in the tenements and on the fire escapes of a crowded city on a hot summer night. The majestic music builds to a dramatic climax that showcases Springsteen's soaring lead guitar. "Rosalita (Come out Tonight)" is the album's other high point, a rollicking, Latin-tinged song in which the singer tries to persuade a girl to slip out of her parents' house for a night of romance, fun, and adventure. Springsteen's exuberant vocals, alternately swaggering and pleading, are the perfect complement to the music, which is dominated by Clarence Clemons's mighty sax.

Springsteen's confidence in the studio had grown considerably, and he had very clear ideas as to how the songs should be arranged and recorded. A tireless perfectionist, he would work endlessly in the studio to realize his ideas. David Sancious recalls, "Bruce works in such a way that whenever he writes a song, he knows exactly how

Bruce Springsteen and Steve Van Zandt enjoy a spontaneous moment in the recording studio. Although Springsteen never tired of experimenting, he had definite ideas of what he wanted to accomplish. Keyboard player David Sancious said, "He knows exactly how he wants it to sound."

he wants it to sound. There's space on there to interpret, but he'll verbally tell you what kind of things he wants."

Unlike the thunderous overpromotion that accompanied the release of *Greetings,* Columbia Records released the second album with virtually no publicity of any kind. There were few advertisements, and no one at the company seemed enthusiastic about the record or committed to making it a success. Many were bewildered by the variety of musical styles it employed, and had no idea how to promote an album containing such a diverse collection of songs. Columbia spent almost no money publicizing the album, leaving it to Springsteen and the band to promote the record through live performances.

Without the customary support from the record company, the new album sold very poorly at first, selling at an even slower rate than *Greetings.* It appeared to be a bigger commercial disaster than Springsteen's first album. *The Wild, the Innocent and the E Street Shuffle* earned rave reviews from the critics, however—it was even named one of the year's 10 best albums in *Rolling Stone,* the most influential magazine in the rock world.

Financially, though, the situation was as bleak as ever. Springsteen and the E Street Band still performed at small clubs and at colleges, which did not pay very much money. Their weekly expenses exceeded their income, with Columbia making up the difference by again advancing money against future earnings just to cover their touring costs. The band members each earned just $35 a week, and Springsteen's total earnings for the year were just over $5,000, a tiny income for an artist who performed almost constantly and who had released two albums on a major record label.

In the early months of 1974, the growing sales figures of *The Wild, the Innocent and the E Street Shuffle* were encouraging, although Laurel Canyon's debt to Columbia was so large that these sales were used to repay the record company and therefore did not result in any additional money for Springsteen. By spring, however, Springsteen was getting engagements in small theaters, which resulted in somewhat larger fees.

By 1974, Springsteen had already developed into a polished and exciting performer. His talents went far beyond a strong, if rough, singing voice and excellent guitar playing. Unlike many rock stars, Springsteen came across as likable and unpretentious, a genuinely nice guy. Bearded and with moderately long hair, he often dressed in T-shirts or work shirts, jeans, and a leather jacket; clearly glamour was not part of his image. A wonderful storyteller, Springsteen's song introductions revealed that he was a keen observer of the humor to be found in even the most mundane situations. Onstage Springsteen was almost constantly in motion, his wiry and athletic body roaming all over the stage, dancing, mugging for the audience, and clowning with his band members. The range of his moods was impressive: passionate, witty, joyous, sorrowful, intense, or goofy, in each situation he seemed honest and sincere.

Bruce Springsteen and the E Street Band spent much of 1974 onstage, performing more than 100 concert dates. By midyear they had graduated from small clubs to theaters and larger nightspots. A growing number of enthusiastic critics, writing in rock publications as well as in general interest magazines and newspapers, championed Springsteen's performances, and many concerts were sold out in advance. No thanks to the still nonexistent promotional efforts of Columbia Records, *The Wild, the Innocent and the E Street Shuffle* received a significant amount of airplay from FM radio stations.

By the middle of 1974, sales of the album passed the 100,000 mark. But because of the immense debt to Columbia for the cost of recording the first two albums, monetary advances for tour costs, and other charges,

Saxophonist Clarence Clemons, drummer Max Weinberg, and Bruce Springsteen perform with the characteristic intensity that earned the E Street Band a reputation as one of the greatest live acts in the history of rock and roll. Springsteen explained his exhausting, high-energy shows, "If I feel I could have given more, it's hard for me to sleep that night."

Springsteen and Laurel Canyon were still a long way from earning any royalties for the sales of the second album. While the gross amounts earned from concerts had grown, so had their expenses. Springsteen's net income for the entire year totaled only $8,500.

His popularity remained greatest around eastern cities, such as New York, Boston, Cleveland, Washington, and especially Philadelphia, but he was no longer only a regional attraction. His summer engagements included successful shows in Arizona and California.

Jim Cretecos, Mike Appel's partner in Laurel Canyon Ltd., grew tired of the constant financial struggles faced by the organization. By early 1974, he had sold his share

68

in the company to Appel for $1,500. Appel carried on as the sole owner of Laurel Canyon and became Springsteen's only manager. The change was slight, as the assertive Appel had always played the dominant role in the arrangement with Springsteen.

The personnel of the E Street Band also underwent some changes. Vini Lopez, who had played with Springsteen for more than five years, was fired in January 1974. Nicknamed Mad Dog because of his fiery temper, Lopez got into frequent fights and simply proved too difficult to control. Despite his long years of service with Springsteen, Lopez was somewhat limited as a drummer, and his sloppy, inconsistent playing was often cited as the band's greatest weakness. Lopez was replaced by Ernest "Boom" Carter, a friend of David Sancious's who was a much more competent drummer than Lopez. (By August, Sancious and Carter would also leave the band, departing with Springsteen's blessing in order to form a new jazz-rock group, Tone, featuring the gifted keyboardist's own adventurous music.)

Springsteen advertised for a new drummer and pianist in the music classified pages of the *Village Voice*, a weekly New York newspaper. After several auditions he settled on drummer Max Weinberg, a talented musician with several years of experience in rock bands as well as in Broadway theater orchestras. To replace Sancious, Springsteen selected pianist Roy Bittan, another skilled musician with formal training and professional credits. Both musicians fit into the E Street Band well, and within a few weeks Springsteen and his musicians were back on the road.

Springsteen made another important connection in 1974. The encounter would prove to be the turning point in his career. Jon Landau, an influential rock critic who wrote for both *Rolling Stone* and the *Boston Phoenix,* had seen Springsteen perform for the first time in April in a

Boston club. Landau was amazed by the performance he witnessed. He wrote a glowing and insightful review of Springsteen's second album, calling it "the most under-rated album so far this year, an impassioned and inspired street fantasy that's as much fun as it is deep." A seasoned writer who had worked as a record producer, he also offered some original and constructive observations on how to improve on some of the record's weaknesses.

Several nights later, Landau returned to the club. His review had been posted on the front window of the building, and as Landau walked up, he recognized a man in a T-shirt who was shivering and hopping around to try to keep warm as he read the review. It was Bruce Spring-steen. Landau asked Springsteen what he thought of the article, and the musician responded that he liked it. Landau introduced himself as the author of the piece, and the two hit it off immediately.

Springsteen returned to Boston a month later, and Landau wrote a review of the show that included the legendary line "I saw rock and roll's future and its name is Bruce Springsteen." Landau, reviewing a performance taking place on the evening of his 27th birthday, went on to say: "And on a night when I needed to feel young, he made me feel like I was hearing music for the very first time." Springsteen and Landau spoke at great length during the singer's stay in Boston, and Springsteen sought the writer's ideas on record production and, in particular, how to improve his own recordings. The two men be-came fast friends and stayed in touch over the next few months, particularly after Landau moved to New York in October.

The Wild, the Innocent and the E Street Shuffle had proved to be a modest success, and there was only a little doubt this time that Columbia wanted another album from Springsteen, although the record company had yet to break even on their investment in the singer. He had written a number of new songs, some of which were performed for months before being discarded without ever having been recorded in favor of more recent compositions. A joyous rocker entitled "Thundercrack" became an audience favorite but never made it to the recording studio.

Springsteen and his musicians returned to 914 Sound Studios, but the sessions were not very productive. Springsteen had grown tired of the technical limitations of the studio. He and the band labored for months between tours and breaks to complete just one song, a powerful new number with a sound that was far different from anything they had previously recorded. Romantic and thrilling, with an arrangement reminiscent of producer Phil Spector's lush, richly textured hits of the early 1960s, it was classic rock and roll, but it managed to sound fresh and new. The song was "Born To Run," and it became an instant classic.

A beautiful and powerful song considered by many to be one of the greatest rock and roll songs ever written, "Born To Run," at four and a half minutes, was about one and a half minutes longer than the average Top 40 hit, and radio programmers at the time usually refused to play records that ran more than four minutes. Columbia Records decided that because of its length, "Born To Run" had no future as a hit single. The record company told Springsteen and Appel to try again. The singer and his manager were crushed, as they felt the song had the potential to bring Springsteen the stardom he had been working toward for almost a decade.

Rather than give up on the idea that "Born To Run" could be a major breakthrough, Mike Appel devised another strategy. If Columbia Records was reluctant to release "Born To Run" to the public, then Appel and Springsteen would have to go around their record company and do the job themselves.

7 "The Promised Land"

MIKE APPEL HAD A SIMPLE, if unusual, plan to bring the song "Born To Run" to the listening public. He sent copies of the song to disc jockeys at FM radio stations who had been particularly supportive of Springsteen's music over the previous year or two. The disc jockeys were all too glad for the opportunity to play Springsteen's hot new song over the air, and when they did the audience response was unbelievably enthusiastic. The song became the most requested record on almost every station that played it, and Springsteen and Appel felt their confidence in the appeal of "Born To Run" had been rewarded. Everyone was pleased, it seemed, except for Columbia Records. The executives there were furious.

Sending "Born To Run" to radio stations long before it would be officially released on an album contradicted the conventional wisdom of the record business. Singles were viewed as a means of attracting the public to buy records—if listeners liked the single, they would be more likely to purchase the album. In this situation, with the album not even close to completion, there was nothing for Columbia Records to sell. It seemed to Columbia that

Much of Bruce Springsteen's appeal stems from his audience's perception of him as a regular guy. This 1982 photograph of Springsteen sitting in a kitchen decorated with framed labels from produce boxes seems to bear out this image.

73

Appel had given away an opportunity of the type that might occur only once or twice in a performer's career.

Appel had, in fact, made a major miscalculation. He had assumed that the album would be completed fairly soon, but this was not the case. One reason for the delay was the familiar problem of 914 Sound Studios's technical deficiencies, but Appel remembers other reasons as well. "Bruce had lost his direction, his energy and to some extent his confidence. We'd been at it for a year, deep in debt to the label, no enthusiasm at CBS for us, continual personnel shifts, so when there were technical breakdowns, it was easy to start shifting the blame as to why things weren't happening."

It was Jon Landau who suggested moving the sessions to the Record Plant, the best-equipped studio in Manhattan—and also one of the most expensive. After struggling with the limitations of 914 Sound Studios for several months, Springsteen was very much in favor of the move. Appel opposed the change, solely for financial reasons, but Springsteen was insistent, and he won the argument. "We went over budget in about two seconds, money that ultimately came out of our pockets," recalled Appel.

Recognizing that Springsteen could yet become a commercial success, Columbia Records agreed to provide the funding to finish the next album at the Record Plant, regardless of the cost. Columbia made this expensive commitment in the interest of completing the recording sessions as quickly as possible and getting the album out to an eager public. For Springsteen and Appel, the record company's unlimited monetary support removed some of the financial pressures for the time being.

Once in the recording studio Springsteen turned to Jon Landau for advice. Springsteen also told Landau that he would never work in the recording studio with Appel again. "There were sounds in his head or ideas in his head that he was unable to capture on tape," Landau remembered. "He said that Mike no more had the solutions to these problems than he did at the moment." Having produced several rock albums, Landau had a deep understanding of the creative process of recording and could provide ideas and solutions that Appel could not.

By February 1975, much to the displeasure of Mike Appel, Jon Landau had joined Springsteen and Appel as a coproducer of the third album. His new coproducer was able to provide the type of assistance in the studio that he had always needed but had never received. The atmosphere in the studio was tense. Appel was largely excluded from the decision-making process. On one occasion, when the tensions were at their highest, Appel was asked to leave the studio by Springsteen and Landau. The banishment was only temporary, but Appel's feelings were hurt, and he grew increasingly resentful of Landau's involvement.

Winter turned to spring, and the recording sessions continued as Springsteen obsessively fine-tuned his songs. Although the band performed infrequently, concerts broadcast over the radio showed that he was still revising the songs even as he was attempting to record them. For example, a wild and unfocused song called "Wings for Wheels" was stripped down to a slow, stark ballad, only to reemerge as the powerful "Thunder Road." An alternate arrangement of "Born To Run," featuring a string orchestra and female backing vocals, was recorded but never released.

Toward the end of the recording sessions, Springsteen and his coproducers were struggling with a version of "Tenth Avenue Freeze-out," a swaggering rhythm and blues tune, when Springsteen had a visitor in the studio. Steve Van Zandt, his old friend and a veteran of several Springsteen bands, looked on as Springsteen and pianist Roy Bittan tried to create parts for the horn section featured on the song. Some of the most talented and expensive session musicians in New York were standing around waiting for direction, but none was forthcoming.

Suddenly Landau had an idea. Landau was aware of Van Zandt's recent involvement, as manager, guitarist, and coleader, with Southside Johnny's new band, the Asbury Jukes, a rhythm and blues group that was earning a reputation as the best bar band on the Jersey Shore. After consulting with Landau, Springsteen pointed at Van Zandt and said, "Okay, Steve, this is the big time."

Discarding the ineffective written music that the session men had been working from, Van Zandt took over the session. Rather than writing out new arrangements for the horn players, Van Zandt created new horn parts on the spot and proceeded to teach each of the musicians his new part by *singing* it to him. Van Zandt's spontaneous horn arrangements were exactly what "Tenth Avenue Freeze-out" needed, and the song was soon completed. Steve Van Zandt, alias Miami Steve, was asked by Springsteen to join the E Street Band as rhythm guitarist and backing vocalist, and he gladly accepted.

The recording and postproduction tasks, such as mixing the multitrack tape and mastering the recording onto vinyl, dragged on and on. At one point Springsteen became so discouraged that he seriously considered discarding much of what had been recorded and replacing it with live versions of the same songs. In August the album was finally finished and ready for release.

To publicize the new album, Appel arranged for Springsteen to play ten shows over five nights in New York, at the Bottom Line. The club had been open only a year, but it had already become a favorite spot to showcase up-and-coming rock and pop performers. The shows, scheduled for August 13–17, were the hottest concert tickets of the summer. Columbia Records purchased about a quarter of the tickets for the entire week,

Springsteen's old friend "Miami" Steve Van Zandt joined the E Street Band in 1975 after an impromptu visit to the recording studio. At the request of coproducer Jon Landau, Van Zandt spontaneously created a vital horn arrangement for the song "Tenth Avenue Freeze-out" on *Born To Run*. Van Zandt later launched a brief solo career as Little Steven.

which were distributed to the press, record company executives, radio programmers, and others in the music industry. The public clamored for the remaining 4,000 tickets, and during the engagement Springsteen fans lined up by early afternoon to purchase standing-room tickets for each evening's performance. The demand for tickets far exceeded the club's 500-seat capacity. Because of the sudden tremendous interest in Springsteen, the early show on the third night was broadcast live on WNEW-FM, the top rock station in New York City, exposing Springsteen to a huge radio audience.

After a somewhat nervous performance on opening night, Springsteen and the E Street Band performed brilliantly for the rest of the week, causing even the cynical music industry figures in the audience to sing his praises. The material from *Born To Run,* which would not be released for more than a week, was received ecstatically. As a result of the acclaim from the press, there was an enormous sense of anticipation regarding the impending appearance of the album.

The songs and performances on *Born To Run* represented another colossal leap forward in Bruce Springsteen's development as an artist. His lyrics exhibited a directness and conciseness that were missing from many of his earlier songs. The album's opening song, "Thunder

Bruce Springsteen and the E Street Band perform at the Bottom Line in New York City in August 1975. The flood of favorable publicity following their 10 electrifying performances there climaxed in October when Springsteen's face appeared simultaneously on the covers of *Time* and *Newsweek* magazines.

Road," begins softly with the sound of Springsteen's harmonica and Roy Bittan's graceful piano. The rest of the band makes its entrance and the music picks up energy and power, like a fast car with its accelerator pressed to the floor. The singer in "Thunder Road" tries to persuade a reluctant young woman to come down off her porch and join him in his car, telling her, "Show a little faith, there's magic in the night." The song perfectly captured the frustration, restless yearning, and exhilarating hope that characterized much of Springsteen's early work.

Though the surging music of "Born To Run" and "Thunder Road" provides the album's powerful center, perhaps the most ambitious song is "Jungleland." Running almost 10 minutes, "Jungleland" has a sophisticated musical arrangement built around Bittan's keyboards, Clemons's sax, and Springsteen's slashing guitar and also uses a violinist and a string orchestra. The music shifts from soft and delicate to loud and rocking before returning to its quieter beginnings, reflecting the sprawling melodrama that is contained in the lyrics. According to rock critic Greil Marcus, *Born To Run* was "like a '57 Chevy running on melted-down Crystals records."

For the first time there was widespread enthusiasm throughout the company for a Springsteen record. They sensed that the album could be a huge commercial success. Columbia Records staged a massive promotional campaign in support of the album, reportedly spending an unprecedented $250,000 in the early months alone.

On August 25 the *Born To Run* album was released, and it became an immediate hit, moving into the top 10 in album sales in its first week. The "Born To Run" single was also a hit, proving that Springsteen and Appel had been correct about the song's appeal despite its four-and-a-half-minute length.

Suddenly Bruce Springsteen's name, voice, and picture seemed to be everywhere. He was a phenomenon, a household name, who in the eyes of many had appeared out of nowhere to become a major rock star. Few knew of the years of struggle Springsteen had survived to reach this point in his career.

Triumphantly, Springsteen and the E Street Band went back on tour, this time more to capitalize on the success of his most recent album than to promote it. Performances in clubs, with only a few exceptions, were a thing of the past because his popularity was so great that he now easily filled theaters and auditoriums of 5,000 seats. In most cases his concerts sold out within hours.

Springsteen and the E Street Band performed better than ever, establishing themselves before new audiences as one of rock's most exciting live acts. The addition of Miami Steve Van Zandt on guitar added a more muscular element to the band's sound, and his impassioned harmony vocals seemed to give greater depth to Springsteen's lead vocals. Max Weinberg on drums provided the solid foundation that the band had lacked during Vini Lopez's tenure. Clarence Clemons continued to supply solid saxophone work and also contributed backing vocals to the band's performances.

Springsteen and his band played in virtually every part of the country and even made a short concert tour of Europe. The four-concert trip to England, Sweden, and the Netherlands was not a complete success, however, despite eager European crowds. Springsteen was in a foul mood because he felt the concerts were crassly overhyped by CBS Records International, which had plastered London with publicity materials and advertisements that recalled the overpromotion surrounding the release of *Greetings* nearly three years earlier. The tour's first show, in London, was reportedly one of the worst performances Springsteen had given in several years. Before the show,

Springsteen reportedly tore down all the signs he could find bearing the by-now nettlesome quotation of Jon Landau's proclaiming him the future of rock and roll.

The culmination of Springsteen's new fame took place on the week of October 27, 1975, when he appeared simultaneously on the covers of both *Time* and *Newsweek,* America's two leading news magazines. Nobody from the entertainment world, let alone a rock star who had been unknown to the general public only months before, had ever pulled off this feat. Normally one magazine's plans to do such a feature would discourage the other from running a similar story. Mike Appel deserved much of the credit for the *Time* and *Newsweek* covers. He had discussed feature articles with both magazines, demanding the front cover for Springsteen in return for granting an interview. But not even Appel expected to land Springsteen on both covers at once.

Having at last achieved the critical and commercial success he had desired for so long, Bruce Springsteen should have been a happy man. In reality he was anything but satisfied; his life was changing in ways that he could not control. Very shortly his unhappiness would endanger everything he had accomplished.

8 "Point Blank"

BRUCE SPRINGSTEEN HAD SEVERAL REASONS to be unhappy. An extremely private man, he found his newfound fame intrusive. Springsteen had always been a loner. He enjoyed playing pinball in an arcade for an hour or two or getting in his car to drive around and listen to music by himself. Now that he had become a star, his life was no longer his own. Interviewers and writers dug into his private affairs. Everyone wanted their piece of Bruce Springsteen, and he missed the anonymity in which he had lived for most of his life.

But these problems were minor in comparison with those he was facing with his career. Despite the success of *Born To Run* and the subsequent tour, Springsteen's earnings remained relatively small. The profits from the album went to Columbia to pay off the massive advances given to Laurel Canyon over the previous three years. As a result of the large sales of *Born To Run* the debt was finally paid, but there was not much left over for distribution to Laurel Canyon, let alone to Springsteen. As of early 1976, Springsteen had not earned a cent from *Born To Run,* an album that had sold around a million copies.

Although *Born To Run* had sold about a million copies by early 1976, Springsteen had not made a dime from the album because of debts and some dubious contracts with his manager, Mike Appel. A legal dispute with Appel would keep Springsteen out of the recording studio for the next year.

Springsteen soon had good reason to question whether Appel had his best interests at heart. After the debt to Columbia was paid, Appel had taken a further advance against earnings from *Born To Run* and future releases in the amount of $500,000. The entire sum went to Laurel Canyon, and none was paid to Springsteen. Because of the contract between the production company and Columbia, this was perfectly legal.

Appel and Springsteen had agreed that when Springsteen became a commercial success they would tear up their original contracts and replace them with ones giving Springsteen a larger percentage of the income from his records, concert tours, and songwriting royalties. Appel did not have to revise the contracts, as they were still legally binding for another year, but he had promised Springsteen that he would. He valued his association with Springsteen and very much wished to see it continue. Appel prepared new contracts with improved terms that would run another five years from the date they were signed. He also said that he would give Springsteen a significant portion of the $500,000 advance when the singer signed the new agreement.

Sensing that something was seriously wrong in his financial relationship with Mike Appel, Springsteen said to Jon Landau, "I am starting to get the feeling that I am not being treated right. I sold close to a million albums. I just toured every big city in the United States. I have $3,000 in the bank right now. Mike received $500,000 from CBS in November. So far I haven't gotten any of it." Landau responded, "That's ridiculous."

Soon Landau was helping Springsteen make sense of his tangled financial situation. Landau provided badly needed advice regarding the negotiation of Springsteen's new contracts with Laurel Canyon. Mike Appel became increasingly resentful of Jon Landau's relationship with Springsteen. He could see that Landau had replaced him

Springsteen's manager, Mike Appel, was a former U.S. marine with a style so belligerent that he alienated many people who could have helped him. For example, when he believed certain disc jockeys were not playing Springsteen's records frequently enough, Appel admitted to sending them coal for Christmas. Some said he also accused them of taking bribes to give preferential treatment to other artists.

as Springsteen's closest friend and professional adviser. When, at Landau's suggestion, Springsteen hired an attorney to review the new contracts, Appel grew angry and defensive. He threatened to hold Springsteen to the terms of the old contract for the remaining year if he did not agree to sign the new one. Appel also threatened to withhold all of the $500,000 advance he had received from Columbia.

In fairness to Appel, it is unlikely that he intended to deny Springsteen his rightful share of his earnings. Appel had invested four years of his life in making Springsteen a star, and now his relationship with Springsteen was being threatened at a time when both men were finally in the position to reap the financial benefits of their hard work. Springsteen was Mike Appel's only client. Appel believed that he was about to lose his most valuable asset, the hottest new star in rock music, and he believed that Jon Landau's interference was the cause.

Appel's response—using Springsteen's existing contract as a bargaining chip—was a typically aggressive
tactic, but it turned Springsteen against Appel forever.
Springsteen was enraged at Appel's efforts to intimidate
him. He felt that he had been betrayed by someone he
had once regarded as one of his closest friends. John
Hammond's prediction that the unfair terms of the contracts signed in 1972 would lead to trouble was about to
prove all too accurate.

On July 27, 1976, Bruce Springsteen sued Mike Appel
and Laurel Canyon Ltd., charging them with a number
of illegalities, including fraud, failure to provide an ac-
counting of Springsteen's income, and misappropriating
funds that were due to Springsteen from Laurel Canyon.
The lawsuit also sought to ensure that Springsteen would
be able to return to the recording studio with Jon Landau
acting as sole producer, an arrangement that could be
blocked under the old contract with Laurel Canyon.
Springsteen also asked for $1,000,000 in damages from
Mike Appel. In short, Springsteen was suing to gain
control over his own career.

But Appel fought back. Two weeks later, as the result
of a separate lawsuit brought by Appel and Laurel Canyon, Springsteen was forbidden from recording with
anyone other than Appel or a producer approved by
Appel. Landau was specifically barred from producing
Springsteen until the dispute was resolved.

For Springsteen, who was ready to capitalize on the
success of *Born To Run,* this ruling was devastating. His
only income came from short concert tours in the fall of
1976 and early 1977. Despite his continuing financial
problems, Springsteen kept all the members of the
E Street Band on salary, whether they were working or
not. This policy not only created great loyalty from the
musicians but also ensured their availability whenever it
was time to rehearse, record, or tour.

Because of his financial difficulties, Springsteen finally agreed to perform two concerts at a large sports arena, the Spectrum in Philadelphia. On the day of the first concert, October 25, 1976, he made a painstaking two-hour sound check in order to provide the best possible sound quality. He also roamed the far reaches of the hall, as the band played onstage, to hear for himself how the music would sound in every corner of the arena.

Despite playing to an audience that was almost five times larger than his usual crowd, Springsteen put on a typically electrifying show, proving that it was possible to stage an arena show without losing the excitement and intensity that had long made his performances so special.

Miami Steve Van Zandt used the period during the lawsuits to continue his work with Southside Johnny and the Asbury Jukes, the band he and Southside Johnny had founded several years earlier. Van Zandt produced the group's first three albums while also contributing guitar and harmony vocals, and he wrote much of their material, including the timeless soul song "I Don't Want To Go Home." Springsteen also contributed songs to each of the three albums, including "The Fever," a soulful ballad that he had written in 1974 but never chose to release. Van Zandt produced some excellent music for Southside Johnny, and the group's connection with Springsteen added much to its popularity. Unfortunately, the band's music was out of step with popular tastes, and the Jukes never became a major attraction.

Springsteen's legal problems continued for almost a year, during which he was legally barred from recording with Landau. Mike Appel had a strong case because he had Springsteen's signature on valid contracts. Also, few of the allegations made by Springsteen in his suit could be proved. But the one thing that Appel valued most, his working relationship with Springsteen, was damaged beyond repair. It was in the interest of both sides to negotiate a settlement.

The court proceedings dragged on until June 1977, when an agreement was finally reached. It would take seven years, however, before Springsteen's career recovered the momentum it had lost. Mike Appel received a large cash settlement, a share of the income and song publishing royalties from Springsteen's first three albums, and a contract from Columbia for Laurel Canyon Ltd. to record new artists for the record label. He released Springsteen from all remaining obligations. Springsteen received his freedom. He could record with any producer and sign with any record label, and he owned all the publishing rights to his songs.

Columbia Records had been very supportive during the law-suits, and Springsteen rewarded its loyalty by signing a contract with the company. No longer was Springsteen the virtual employee of his own manager. Jon Landau, his trusted friend and adviser, became Springsteen's new manager, but Springsteen

had learned his lesson and would no longer play a passive role in directing his own career.

By June 1977, Bruce Springsteen and the E Street Band were finally back in the recording studio, with Springsteen and Landau sharing production duties. Springsteen's high standards in the studio once again prolonged the recording process. His fourth album, *Darkness on the Edge of Town,* was finally released on

A grinning Bruce Springsteen is flanked by lawyer Peter Tannen (left) and his friend Jon Landau. In 1976, after Springsteen settled his lawsuit with his estranged manager, Mike Appel, Landau became both his manager and producer.

June 2, 1978, nearly three years after the appearance of *Born To Run.* Although the album did not receive the overwhelming attention of its predecessor, *Darkness* was much anticipated by Springsteen's loyal fans, and it became a big seller.

In addition to the triumphant opening song, "Badlands," *Darkness* contains two other masterpieces: "The Promised Land," a strong folk-rock song with an angry edge, and the title tune. In "Darkness on the Edge of Town," as in "Badlands," the singer is a man who has lost what little he has ever had in life but finds a reason to struggle on.

Darkness is an angry album. The romantic optimism that characterized much of *Born To Run* is gone. The songs no longer promise triumph; instead they pledge survival. As Springsteen said, "There's less of a sense of a free ride than there is on *Born To Run.* There's more a sense of: If you wanna ride, you're gonna pay."

Although the subject matter on *Darkness* is sometimes depressing, the songs are moving and believable. The characters remain defiant and undefeated, despite the realization that few of their dreams have come true. Springsteen himself stated that "*Darkness* is about dealing with despair, about people trying to hold on to their dignity in the middle of a hurricane. You look around, you see people on the street dug in. You know they're already six feet under, people with nothin' to lose and full of poison. I try to write about the other choice they've got."

Reviews of *Darkness on the Edge of Town* were very positive. Dave Marsh in *Rolling Stone* wrote: "Springsteen has been known principally for his songwriting ability, but these songs not only take the writing to a new level but establish him as a major vocalist and guitarist as well." Marsh wrote the first major biography of Springsteen, *Born To Run,* a year later.

The seven-month tour that followed the release of *Darkness* established Springsteen as the biggest attraction in rock. He performed songs from all four of his albums, as well as the oldies that had always been a popular part of his shows, which usually appeared as an encore at the end of the concert. Always a prolific songwriter, Springsteen continued to write new songs throughout the tour, and he introduced several excellent new compositions onstage.

His performances usually lasted more than three hours, twice as long as the average rock concert. Every night Springsteen performed as if it were the most important concert of his life, and the energy and emotion he invested was apparent to every member of the audience. After the last song, usually "Rosalita," Springsteen and the band would leave the stage to a tremendous ovation and resounding cries of "Brooooooce!" Then the musicians would return for two or three encores, which often lasted another 20 or 30 minutes or more.

In the early part of 1979, Springsteen took a much deserved rest before starting work on his next album. Miami Steve Van Zandt joined Springsteen and Landau as a coproducer. While the recording sessions continued, Springsteen accepted an invitation to perform at two benefit concerts organized by a group of concerned musicians called Musicians United for Safe Energy (MUSE). MUSE had formed in 1979 in response to growing concern about the danger posed by nuclear power. It was felt that the high public visibility of rock, folk, and other pop performers would attract a large audience to the No Nukes movement.

The concerts were held at New York's Madison Square Garden in September 1979. On both nights that he performed, Springsteen closed the show, in recognition of his status as the most popular artist on the bill. Though most of the crowd was appreciative of the other performers on the program, it was clear that a large percentage of the crowd was there to see Springsteen, and he did not disappoint them. His riveting performance was captured on film in *No Nukes.*

Released in October 1980, Springsteen's fifth album, *The River,* was a two-record set. As usual, he had written a great number of new songs, but this time he chose to record and release a larger portion of his new material. The 20 songs on *The River* cover a surprisingly wide range of moods and musical styles.

The River has several effective, high-energy rockers, such as "The Ties that Bind," "Two Hearts," "Out in the Street," "You Can Look (But You Better Not Touch)," and "Cadillac Ranch." "Sherry Darling" is a funny, almost nostalgic rock and roll tune reminiscent of the raucous early 1960s hits of Gary "U.S." Bonds. Yet perhaps the most interesting songs on *The River* are three very dark and intense tunes. "Independence Day," a bittersweet song in which the singer is making peace with his father on the eve of leaving home, seemingly includes parallels to Springsteen's relationship with his own father. "Point Blank," an angry song about a failed relationship in which the singer condemns his ex-girlfriend for giving up on him and on herself, is one of Springsteen's most haunting compositions. The title song is another moving story in which possibilities seem to steadily dwindle with the passage of time, like the river that had always flowed through the singer's hometown but had finally run dry.

The River also contains the brief, catchy tune "Hungry Heart," which became Springsteen's first top-10 hit. Springsteen had always resisted submitting to the commercial requirements of the rock industry, refusing to alter his style and message for what he viewed as a crass attempt to make money, and some of his longtime fans accused him of selling out with the pop-oriented "Hungry Heart." But Springsteen's discovery that he could

Bruce Springsteen sits at the feet of his longtime bandmate Clarence Clemons during a 1985 performance. The rapport between the two musicians added an extra dimension to the feeling of camaraderie at Springsteen's concerts. One regular feature of the show was a dramatic kiss between Springsteen and Clemons.

maintain his integrity while adapting to reach a mass audience would prove a turning point in his career, not unlike his reluctant decision a few years before to bring his shows to large arenas.

In October 1980, Springsteen launched a five-month tour, and as in 1978, not a ticket went unsold. Soon afterward, Springsteen began a two-month European tour—his first concerts in Europe since his short and stormy visit there promoting *Born To Run*. Springsteen and the E Street Band received ecstatic responses from audiences everywhere they performed in Europe.

The respect with which the European audiences greeted not just his music but his spoken comments seemed to give Springsteen the confidence to address broader social issues. Through long discussions with Jon Landau, who, recognizing a fellow intellectual, had suggested a number of books to read, Springsteen finally began to give himself the education he had never bothered to acquire in school. His reading helped put in perspective a lot of things his own family had experienced.

In England Springsteen mused onstage, "I started reading this book, *The History of the United States,* and it seemed that things weren't the way they were meant to be—like the way my old man was living, and his old man, and the life that was waiting for me—that wasn't the original idea."

During a concert in Paris he told the audience,

I grew up in this house where there was never any books or I guess anything that was considered art or anything. And I remember when I was in school, at the time . . . I just wasn't interested.

But when I got older I looked back and I saw that my father, he quit high school and went in the army and he got married real young and picked up jobs where he could, workin' in a factory, driving a truck. And I look back at my grandfather and he worked at a rug mill in the town that I grew up in. And it seemed like we all had one thing in common and that was that we didn't know enough, we didn't know about what was happening to us. Like, I'm 31 now and I just started to read the history of the United States. And the thing about it is, I started to learn about how things got to be the way they are today, how you end up a victim without even knowing it. And how people get old and just die after not having hardly a day's satisfaction or peace of mind in their lives.

I was lucky, too, because I met this guy, when I was in my middle twenties, who said you should watch this or you should read this. And most people, where I come from, never have someone try and help them in that way. So all I'm sayin' is, is try to learn, learn about yourselves, learn about who you are now. And try to make it better.

In July 1981, Springsteen and the E Street Band performed six consecutive sold-out performances at the Brendan Byrne Arena, the opening event at a new sports arena that had opened at the Meadowlands, a massive complex in East Rutherford, New Jersey, a few miles across the Hudson River from New York City. The engagement had the mood of a homecoming, as Springsteen returned to his home state to perform before adoring crowds every night. The demand for tickets was so great that it was estimated that he could have played at the Byrne Arena every night for a month without satisfying every ticket request.

During the *Darkness* tour in 1978, Springsteen had read *Born on the Fourth of July,* a remarkable book by Vietnam veteran Ron Kovic. Kovic had gone to Vietnam as a patriotic member of the U.S. Marine Corps; he returned paralyzed from the waist down. Kovic soon grew disillusioned by the treatment he and other veterans had received upon their return and became a leading spokesman for Vietnam veterans. Many veterans of the war suffered from physical or psychological problems related to their Vietnam experience, while others suffered from addictions to drugs or alcohol. Yet the Veterans Administration did little to help these younger veterans with their problems. The U.S. government and most of the American public were eager to forget the nightmare of Vietnam.

Springsteen was deeply moved by Kovic's book, and his memories of Bart Haines, the Castiles' drummer who had died tragically in the Vietnam War, made his response to the book that much stronger. Springsteen decided that he wanted to help the Vietnam veterans in some way. Through Jon Landau, Springsteen contacted the leaders of Vietnam Veterans of America (VVA), an organization formed to further the interests of those who had served in the conflict. The organization had almost no money and was struggling for survival.

Springsteen offered to perform a benefit concert for the VVA. The sold-out concert took place in Los Angeles on August 20, 1981. Speaking to a huge audience that included dozens of disabled veterans sitting in wheelchairs in a section that had been built especially for them, Springsteen nervously made the first overtly political speech of his career.

> Tonight we're here for the men and the women that fought in the Vietnam War. Yesterday I was lucky enough and I met some of these guys [disabled veterans]. And it was funny, because I'm used to comin' out in front of a lot of people and I realized that I was nervous and I was a little embarrassed about not knowin' what to say to 'em.
>
> And it's like when you feel like you're walkin' down a dark street at night and out of the corner of your eye you see somebody gettin' hurt or somebody gettin' hit in the dark alley but you keep walkin' on because you think it don't have nothin' to do with you and you just wanna get home.
>
> Well, Vietnam turned this whole country into that dark street. And unless we're able to walk down those dark alleys and look into the eyes of the men and the women that are down there and the things that happened, we're never gonna be able to get home . . . and then it's only a chance.

You guys! You guys out there that are eighteen and nineteen years old—it happened once and it can happen again.

VVA president Bob Muller, a 36-year-old paraplegic veteran who became good friends with Springsteen, said, "Without Bruce and that evening, we would not have made it. We would have had to close down." At a time when the VVA was in desperate straits, the concert raised almost $250,000 for the organization and gave it national visibility. It is Muller's opinion that "without Bruce Springsteen, there would be no Vietnam veterans movement."

9 "Glory Days"

AFTER AN EXHAUSTING 1981, SPRINGSTEEN began to put together material for his next album. As usual, he had many songs from which to choose. The recording sessions began in the spring of 1982 in New York, and in the first three weeks he and the E Street Band had recorded half an album's worth of material, much of it upbeat rock and roll tunes. Everybody was pleased with both the quality of the music and the rapid pace at which the recordings were being completed, except Springsteen. He had another group of songs on his mind, and at the moment they seemed much more important to him.

Springsteen had spent a large part of the preceding year listening to classic American artists whom he had never taken the time to listen to previously. These included such important singer-songwriters as Woody Guthrie, a folksinger who had recorded primarily in the 1940s, and Hank Williams, a country singer whose greatest success came in the early 1950s. Singing simple yet powerful songs about everyday lives, Guthrie and Williams were both master storytellers who communicated with an honesty and sincerity that is

---

Springsteen's music displayed a growing social consciousness with the 1982 album *Nebraska* and the 1984 smash hit *Born in the U.S.A.* Here he performs acoustically at a 1987 benefit concert for New York City's homeless.

99

almost unique in popular music. Springsteen was moved
by the power of their music and at how effectively they
delivered their messages. The directness of Guthrie's and
Williams's songwriting styles was an inspiration to
Springsteen, and he soon applied a similar directness to
his own writing.

Using an inexpensive four-track cassette tape recorder
and accompanying himself on guitar and harmonica,
Springsteen recorded demos of these new songs, intending for the band to record more elaborate versions of the
tunes during their recording sessions. On January 3,
1982, Springsteen recorded approximately 15 songs in
renditions that were stark and dramatic, but utterly con-
vincing. In the next few days he mixed the tracks onto a
single tape.

Springsteen brought the songs to the recording sessions, but his attempts to record the tunes with the full
band were largely unsuccessful. He was extremely frus-
trated, as the songs were very important to him, and
everyone who heard his demo tape agreed that it represented a new and important direction in his work. Springsteen refused to give up on the songs, yet the versions
attempted in the studio failed to capture the strengths of
the demo. It was a discouraging situation. Thinking out
loud, Jon Landau turned to Springsteen and said, "Well,
we can just put the demo out the way it is." Springsteen
looked at his friend; he had been thinking exactly the
same thing but had been afraid to say it.

Releasing an album consisting of Bruce singing quietly
to himself with no accompaniment except his own guitar
and harmonica would be risky and controversial. At a
time when the pop music charts were dominated by
records featuring electronic synthesizers and heavy-metal
guitars, Springsteen's decision to put out an almost entirely acoustic album raised more than a few eyebrows.
On top of that, the subject matter of the songs was

extremely disturbing, if not downright depressing. For example, "Nebraska," which would become the title song, is a first-person account of an unrepentant mass murderer who faces death in the electric chair. No matter how big a star Springsteen had become, it seemed unlikely that this music could reach a large audience. There was some resistance from Columbia Records, but Springsteen and Landau were insistent. In the end Columbia agreed to release the album exactly as it was.

Turning the demo tape into a finished album was not as easy as it seemed. The tape was poorly recorded, and the tape recorder Springsteen had used had several technical problems that were difficult to overcome. Transferring the songs to a studio quality master tape proved extremely difficult. Both Springsteen and his sound engineer, Chuck Plotkin, struggled for several months until they were at the point of giving up, a prospect Springsteen found devastating. But finally they succeeded in creating a master and were able to cut a record.

Nebraska was released to a somewhat confused public in September 1982, many of whom wondered why one of the greatest rock stars of his generation had released what was, essentially, a folk album with rather depressing subject matter. His loyal fans bought the album anyway, and most came to appreciate the power of the songs. The album sold reasonably well, although substantially less than *The River.* The critical response was positive; Robert Palmer of the *New York Times* called *Nebraska* "an austere, compelling and cost-efficient state-of-the-union message."

In the 1980s, everyday life was becoming a struggle for many working-class Americans. President Ronald Reagan and the Republicans who had come to power in 1981 seemed intent on reducing the government assistance that was available to America's poor in the interest of reducing taxes and government expenditures. While some Americans would prosper under these conditions, many others found that their lives grew more and more difficult. Factories closed, often forever, and millions of working-class families did not know where to turn for help. Families that had worked hard all their lives were losing their homes, were going to bed hungry, or were going without medical care because they had no health insurance. Those Americans who were struggling for their survival desperately needed a public voice, and Springsteen's quiet album spoke for them.

Springsteen's examination of the broken lives on *Nebraska* went deeper than superficial political issues, probing instead the spiritual crisis of a society in which the bonds that held the members of the community together were dissolving. Praising Springsteen's uncompromising message, critic Mikal Gilmore of the *Los Angeles Herald Examiner* wrote: "A dark-toned, brooding and unsparing record, *Nebraska* is also the most successful attempt at making a sizable statement about American life that popular music has yet produced."

The album's title tune, a chilling song based on an actual event, tells the story of Charles Starkweather, a young man who goes on a murder spree in which he takes 10 innocent lives. When he is captured, tried for his crimes, and condemned to die, he feels no remorse for his violent deeds: "They wanted to know why I did what I did / Well, sir, I guess there's just a meanness in this world."

"Highway Patrolman" is another disturbing song, about two brothers who live in a small Michigan town. The narrator is an honest cop whose brother is "no good." As his brother works his way deeper and deeper into trouble, the cop is torn between his duty as an officer and his loyalty to his brother. "Man turns his back on his family," the cop concludes. "Well, he just ain't no good."

Soon after the completion of *Nebraska,* Springsteen and the band returned to the studio to finish recording the album he had begun during the *Nebraska* sessions. There was one major change, however. Apparently with Springsteen's blessing and encouragement, Steve Van Zandt left the E Street Band to pursue a solo career.

Calling his new band Little Steven and the Disciples of Soul, Van Zandt recorded a soul-music-inflected album of his own songs. The material on *Men Without Women* was as solid as anything he had written for Southside Johnny, and the group featured a number of excellent musicians. There was one major problem, however. Unfortunately, Steve Van Zandt was not a good singer, even by rock's undemanding standards. His hoarse and strained voice made even his best songs difficult to listen to. Van Zandt's vocal limitations had never been a problem when he was supporting stronger vocalists like Springsteen or Southside Johnny, but on his own, his shortcomings were all too obvious. A second, more hard rock–oriented album that was released in 1984, *Voice of America,* suffered from the same fatal flaw.

Springsteen and the E Street Band finished the next album, which was entitled *Born in the U.S.A.,* and prepared it for release in 1984. Much more rock oriented than *Nebraska,* it was expected to be a much bigger hit. But no one was prepared for what occurred when the new recording was issued. *Born in the U.S.A.* not only became a hit, it became one of the top-selling albums of all time.

Born in the U.S.A. sold approximately 21 million copies worldwide, roughly 10 times the amount of Springsteen's previous best-seller, *The River.* It contains both upbeat rockers and slower, reflective ballads that offer some of the most memorable melodies and musical arrangements he had ever written. Of the seven hit singles that were released, Springsteen scored seven top-10 hits. "My Hometown" was used as the theme music for the

Bruce Springsteen performs at one of the concerts in his record-breaking tour following his 1984 album *Born in the U.S.A.* The tour sold 5 million tickets in all, and the album sold 21 million copies and spawned 7 top-10 hits.

telecast of the 1984 World Series, and Chrysler reportedly offered Springsteen $12 million to use "Born in the U.S.A." in a commercial. (When Springsteen refused, a jingle company was hired to write an imitation, and before long country music star Kenny Rogers was wailing "The pride is back, born in America" for Chrysler.)

The single "Dancing in the Dark" was released first, accompanied by Springsteen's first big-budget music video (a video had been released for one of *Nebraska's* songs, but Springsteen did not appear in the video, and it had little impact on sales). The "Dancing in the Dark" video, directed by Brian De Palma, one of the first Hollywood directors to make a music video, was an attempt to sell Springsteen's music via the cable television network MTV. "Dancing in the Dark" became a major hit on MTV, and both the single and the album received a significant amount of radio airplay as well. Sales of the *Born in the U.S.A.* album were tremendous from the first day of its release, and the recording moved to the top of the sales charts.

The last song written and recorded for the album, "Dancing in the Dark" alienated some longtime fans, who were distressed by the song's commercial, dance-oriented music, which seemed calculated to make the song a pop hit. But the bouncy rhythm and insistent synthesizer of "Dancing in the Dark" perhaps make the song sound happier than it was meant to be. The cheerful video also obscured the feeling of isolation expressed by the lyrics.

In the album's angry title song, the singer returns from Vietnam to find that no one acknowledges the sacrifices he has made and that he cannot even get a job. A powerful, mesmerizing song and performance, "Born in the U.S.A." was somehow misinterpreted by some listeners to be a patriotic song, but this was definitely not Springsteen's intended meaning. The singer repeats the title phrase over and over, almost defiantly, as if to remind himself that he belongs in the country, even though he has received so little in return for his contributions to his homeland. He has not just been disappointed, he has been betrayed by the system, and he is furious. The anger of the lyrics is matched by the music, which is dominated by the trumpetlike call of Roy Bittan's synthesizer and Max Weinberg's explosive drumming.

"Glory Days" is an upbeat but wistful look backward at vanishing youth and faded dreams. It features Steve Van Zandt's prominent vocals and mandolin solo, roles that he reprised in the song's video. The departure of Van Zandt, his old friend, from the E Street Band was seemingly on Springsteen's mind when he wrote and recorded "No Surrender" and "Bobby Jean," two songs preoccupied with old friendship that exhibit both warmth and sadness.

With Steve Van Zandt's departure, the E Street Band underwent its first personnel changes in almost a decade. Replacing Van Zandt was Nils Lofgren, a talented guitarist and vocalist who had had a long solo career. Lofgren and Springsteen had met in 1969 when Steel Mill first visited San Francisco. The two musicians had kept in contact over the years while Lofgren worked with Neil Young and a band called Grin before embarking on his solo career. After some early successes, Lofgren had struggled, and in early 1984 he called Springsteen to offer his services as Van Zandt's replacement. Another addition to the E Street Band was Patti Scialfa, a young veteran of the Asbury Park music scene who had previously worked with Southside Johnny. Scialfa joined the group as a backup vocalist.

To break in the new players, Springsteen and the revamped E Street Band played several unadvertised warmup shows at the Stone Pony, the most popular club in Asbury Park. It had been Springsteen's habit for some years to show up at the club unannounced and sit in with the featured performer, something he also did periodically in other towns as well.

Springsteen and the E Street Band began the "Born in the U.S.A." tour in June 1984, and they would remain on the road, with a few breaks, for 16 months. Because of his increased popularity, it was not practical for Springsteen to perform at the 20,000-seat arenas where he had been appearing since 1976. Instead many of the concerts had to be held in baseball or football stadiums that seated more than 50,000 fans. In many cities Springsteen still performed over several nights to accommodate the intense demand for tickets. Because of the immense distance from the stage to the far reaches of the stadiums, large video screens were used to project the performance to the crowd. There was no longer even the illusion of intimacy in these large stadiums, but the video screens at least enabled everyone to follow the action onstage.

Although many of Springsteen's longtime fans still attended his concerts, there were many others who were attracted by the success of *Born in the U.S.A.* and were experiencing their first Springsteen performances. Many of the new fans cared little for the stories and spoken introductions that had long been a part of Springsteen's concerts. They showed even less patience whenever he spoke out briefly on social issues. Attracted only by his upbeat rock tunes, many of the new fans talked, shouted, whistled, and whooped during the concerts' quieter moments. The rudeness and disrespect of the new fans shocked both Springsteen and his older fans because he had long received the complete respect and attention of his audiences.

The *Born in the U.S.A.* tour played before more people than any other concert tour in history, performing to a total audience of about five million. The tour earned about $100 million from ticket sales alone, which was also a record. The *Born in the U.S.A.* album spent a year near the top of the sales charts. Springsteen's tours of Europe, Asia, and Australia in 1985 were also big successes, his concerts filling soccer stadiums and other large outdoor venues.

Springsteen's popularity was so great in 1984 that both major political parties attempted to use the singer's name and image in the presidential race. Spokespeople

On August 6, 1985, Bruce Springsteen sings before a sold-out crowd at R.F.K. Memorial Stadium in Washington, D.C. Springsteen's *Born in U.S.A.* tour became the highest grossing concert tour in rock history, taking in approximately $100 million in tickets sales. At reach city, however, he donated money to local organizations, such as food banks, and urged his audience to become more involved in their communities.

for the Republican party attempted to portray Springsteen as a champion of traditional American patriotism, which was a total misrepresentation of his views. President Ronald Reagan, while campaigning in New Jersey for his reelection, said, "America's future rests in a thousand dreams inside your hearts; it rests in the message of hope in songs so many young Americans admire: New Jersey's own Bruce Springsteen. And helping you make those dreams come true is what this job of mine is all about."

Springsteen reluctantly responded, "I didn't know whether to be embarrassed for me or for the President." Several days later, while onstage, he offered further comment: "The President was mentioning my name the other day, and I kinda got to wondering what his favorite album musta been. I don't think it was the *Nebraska* album."

Because of the enormous success of both the *Born in the U.S.A.* album and tour, Springsteen was becoming a very wealthy man. He bought a large home in Rumson, New Jersey, one of the state's prettiest areas, and also bought a home in Los Angeles. But he shared his wealth with others as well. In most cities where he performed, Springsteen made sizable contributions to local food banks, organizations set up to feed the needy. He also made donations to other causes, including medical clinics and strike funds for workers involved in labor disputes. Springsteen considered himself an artist, not a politician, but he had no intention of being used as a political football by others who wished to invoke his image. Rather than criticizing President Reagan head-on, Springsteen made his feelings known far more constructively. He distanced himself from Reagan by drawing attention to those who had been hurt by the president's policies and by asking his fans to support their local unions and food banks at his concerts. In 1985, Springsteen also donated his vocal services for "We Are the World," an all-star benefit record made to raise funds for famine relief in Africa, and to *Sun City*, a record put together by Steve Van Zandt to combat the racist policy of apartheid in South Africa.

During one of the tour's several breaks, Springsteen shocked both his friends and fans by getting married. Springsteen had had several serious romantic involvements over the years. But he had always avoided marriage, partly because his music had always been the highest priority in his life and he had not felt ready to make the changes in his lifestyle that would be necessary if he were to marry.

Springsteen had met Julianne Phillips, a beautiful 25-year-old model and actress, in October 1984. The two soon became romantically involved, and Phillips flew to visit Springsteen several times while he was on tour. Amid

Bruce Springsteen and Julianne Phillips appear at the Rock and Roll Hall of Fame Awards in January 1988. The two were married in a secret ceremony in May 1985, but they divorced in 1988. Springsteen later admitted, "It was tough. I didn't really know how to be a husband. She was a terrific person, but I just didn't know how to do it."

great secrecy, Springsteen and Phillips were married in her parents' hometown in Oregon in May 1985.

When the *Born in the U.S.A.* tour ended in Los Angeles on October 2, 1985, it brought to a conclusion one of the longest and most profitable tours in rock history. In the previous 16 months, Springsteen had become one of the biggest stars in the entertainment industry, amassing a fortune that was estimated to be more than $50 million. Springsteen took a much needed and much deserved break and began to build a new life with his bride.

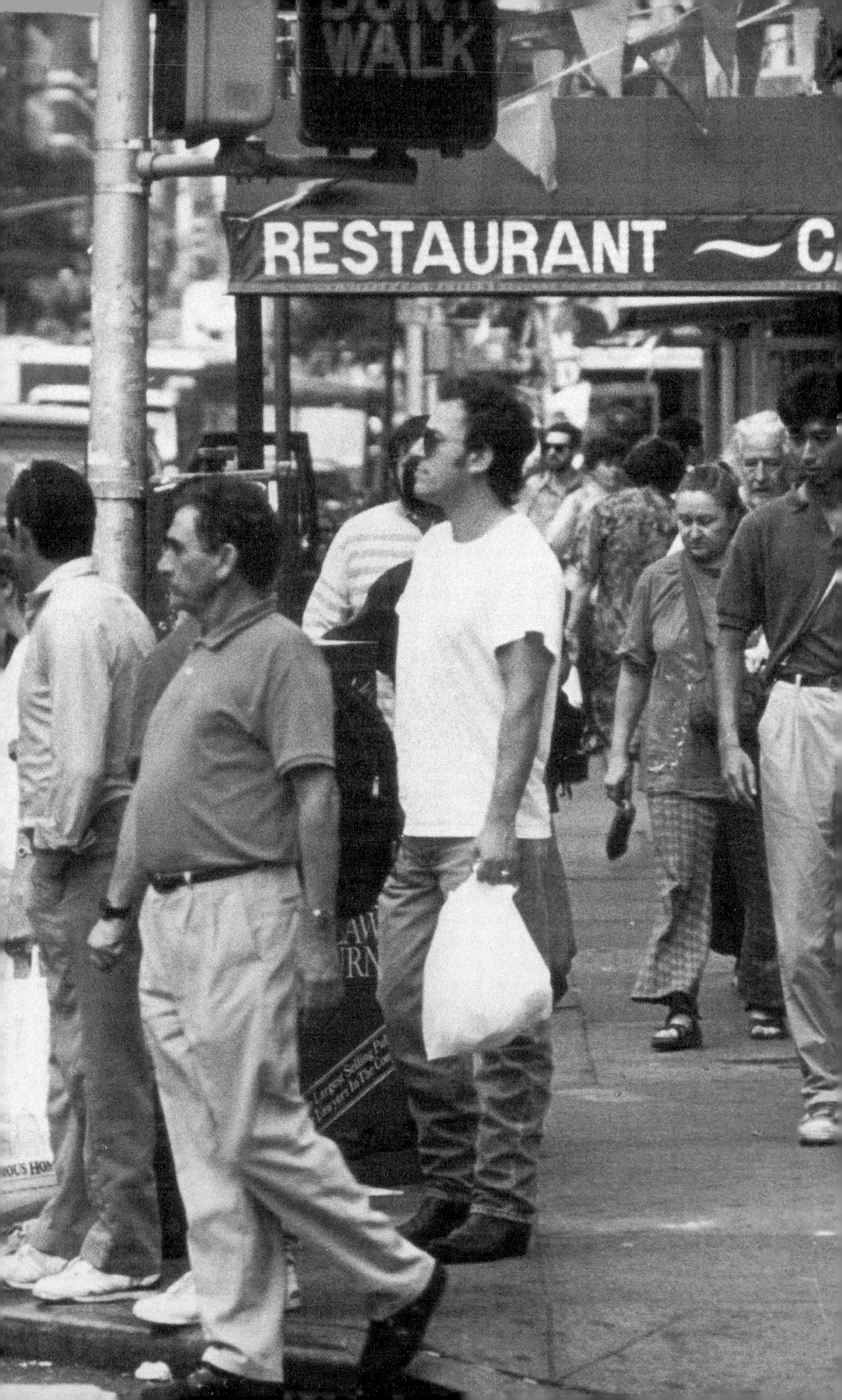
WALK
RESTAURANT

10 "Better Days"

THE ONLY MAJOR PROJECT on Bruce Springsteen's schedule in 1986 was to put together a live album. The notion of releasing a concert recording had been considered as early as 1975, when Mike Appel suggested it as the follow-up release to *Born To Run*. Springsteen rejected the idea at the time, and despite regular requests from his fans and the widespread popularity of numerous illegal bootleg recordings, he gave no serious consideration to a live album for almost a decade. But after the *Born in the U.S.A.* tour, Springsteen and Landau began to put together a comprehensive collection of material covering every period of Springsteen's career.

Several Springsteen concerts had been recorded since the *Born To Run* tour for possible use as live albums, and by the end of 1985 there were hundreds of hours of live music on tape. Landau and Springsteen, working with Chuck Plotkin, listened to every tape, slowly and methodically assembling a collection of strong performances.

Most of Springsteen's best-known songs were included on the album, but the collection also included concert favorites that had never before been released. These included Springsteen's moving version of Woody Guthrie's

In 1991, Bruce Springsteen (center) stands unnoticed on a street corner in New York City. Springsteen now lives in a suburb of Los Angeles, California, because, he says, "Los Angeles provides a lot of anonymity. . . . People wave to you and say hi, but you're pretty much left to go your own way."

classic "This Land Is Your Land"; "Because the Night," a Springsteen song that had been recorded in a slightly different version by punk-rock singer Patti Smith; and "Fire," a Springsteen composition that had been recorded by both rockabilly singer Robert Gordon and the Pointer Sisters. (Springsteen had originally written "Fire" for Elvis Presley, and he even sent Presley a tape of the song in hopes that Presley would record it. One can easily imagine Presley's sensual voice crooning the slow, sultry lyrics.)

The live album was released on five records or three compact discs or cassettes and ran about three hours, which was then considered unusually long even for a career retrospective. It was prepared in almost complete secrecy, and there was no publicity until shortly before its release. Entitled *Live/1975–85,* the album provided an effective overview of Springsteen's career, demonstrating for those who had never experienced one of his concerts why he was considered rock's greatest live performer. The album was released as a boxed set, which included a booklet containing the songs' lyrics and rare photographs. Despite the relatively high cost of the package, *Live/1975–85* was a phenomenal seller.

Springsteen then began work on his next album, much of which was recorded in his home studio with his own overdubbed accompaniment and with only occasional support from members of the E Street Band. *Tunnel of Love* was released in October 1987 and represented another major change of direction in his music. The songs were soft and intimate, and there were none of the upbeat rock tunes that had made *Born in the U.S.A.* popular with such a large audience. The subdued mood of the album seemed like a deliberate reaction against his great popularity with the younger rock fans who had made both *Born in the U.S.A.* and *Live/1975–85* such enormous sellers.

Tunnel of Love is one of Springsteen's most serious albums, focusing on the complex and often frustrating nature of adult relationships. On "Brilliant Disguise," Springsteen paints a picture of a man deeply mistrustful not only of his lover's true feelings and intentions, but of his own as well.

The downbeat mood of the album seemed odd for an artist who had been married for only two years. Unfortunately, the themes of *Tunnel of Love* appear to provide a revealing glimpse into Springsteen's personal life. In early 1988, after only three years of marriage, he and Julianne Phillips filed for divorce. Although he refused to speak publicly on the subject, Springsteen was reportedly devastated by the failure of his marriage.

In September 1988, Springsteen and his band took part in the Human Rights Now! tour, which featured other leading rock acts, such as Sting, Peter Gabriel, and Tracy Chapman. The performers staged a series of major international concerts to raise money for Amnesty International, a nonprofit organization dedicated to freeing political prisoners around the world. The Human Rights Now! tour played to massive crowds and provided desperately needed funding for the human rights group.

The tour's last concert, in October 1988 in Buenos Aires, Argentina, was a historic event, although no one realized it at the time. It was probably the last performance by Bruce Springsteen with the E Street Band. A year later, at his California home, he thanked each of the band members for all the music and memories they had shared. He told them that he needed a change and that they were free to accept other offers. Springsteen, though, did not rule out the possibility that they would work together again someday. Springsteen stayed out of the public view for the next few years, surfacing occasionally to perform at a benefit concert or at the induction ceremonies for the Rock and Roll Hall of Fame.

In Springsteen's personal life, however, there were some major developments. He had become romantically involved with singer Patti Scialfa, the Asbury Park native who had been a member of the E Street Band in its last years. Their relationship seemed to provide Springsteen with the stability and commitment that had always

In September 1988, Bruce Springsteen (far left) performs at the Human Rights Now! concert in London, England, along with (from left to right) Tracy Chapman, Youssou N'Dour, Sting, a backing singer, and Peter Gabriel. Springsteen later said of his life in 1988, "I was kind of wandering and lost, and it was Patti's patience and understanding that got me through. She's a real friend, and we have a real great friendship."

escaped him. Scialfa gave birth to their first child on July 25, 1990, a son named Evan James Springsteen, and on December 30, 1991, the couple had a daughter named Jessica Rae. Springsteen and Scialfa were married in April 1991 in California at their home in the Hollywood Hills. For most of his life, raising a family had seemed

inconceivable, but when he finally settled down Springsteen cherished the experience.

Springsteen, however, did not turn his back on his music. He returned to the recording studio in Los Angeles, and, working with pianist Roy Bittan and hired musicians, recorded an album entitled *Human Touch*. Shortly after its completion, he began working on a new set of songs, recorded at his home studio. Springsteen played almost all the instruments, although he did use a drummer and other guest musicians, including Bittan, on some songs. Soon he had completed a second album, which he called *Lucky Town*.

Human Touch and *Lucky Town* were both released on the last day of March 1992. Initially it seemed that any fears of decreased sales caused by the simultaneous release were unjustified, as the albums debuted at the second and third spots on the sales charts. After several weeks of strong sales, however, both albums quickly dropped from the charts, and in terms of the number of records sold, the two releases were a major disappointment.

The reviews of the two albums were as mixed as any Springsteen had received since early in his career. The critics found much to admire in each collection, but many felt that some of the songs were tame and uninspired, lacking the passion that had long been characteristic of Springsteen's best music. The turbulent emotions that drove his earlier records seemed to be missing from his new work. Reviewer Jon Pareles, writing in the *New York Times,* observed that "Springsteen is starting to sound like a man wrapped up in private preoccupations, running in circles." In a 1992 interview with *Rolling Stone,* Springsteen said that he was indeed coming out of a period of intense introspection. Describing a feeling of isolation that he had struggled with all his life, he said that he had sought therapy and finally felt like a whole person, not just a performer.

Even if no new ground is broken artistically, there are some outstanding songs on the two albums. On *Human Touch,* the more upbeat and rock-oriented of the two albums, the title tune and several others rank with his most powerful work, but with a moodier, more intro-spective focus. The softer and more contemplative *Lucky Town* features such excellent performances as "Leap of Faith," "My Beautiful Reward," and "Better Days," in which he effectively conveys the joy and satisfaction that had now become a part of his life. *Human Touch* and *Lucky Town* reflect the concerns and values of a man who has reached the middle of his life. *Human Touch*'s "All or Nothin' at All" and "Man's Job," for example, proudly describe the challenges and joys of commitment to a long-term relationship.

Bruce Springsteen toured the United States and Europe in the summer of 1992 in support of his two newest albums. To many longtime fans it was a shock to see him perform without the E Street Band, which had shared the stage with Springsteen for almost 20 years. Only keyboard player Roy Bittan remained from his old band, and except for his wife, Patti Scialfa, the rest of the musicians were newcomers.

Musically the new and nameless band was professional and talented, but it lacked some of the special qualities of the E Street Band. Clarence Clemons's sound and stage presence in particular were sorely missed. The band did, however, feature a chorus of five background singers, an unusual touch that added an effective rhythm and blues and gospel sound to some of the songs. But audiences missed the obvious camaraderie and rapport that Spring-steen had shared with the E Street Band.

After the tour ended, Springsteen and his new band taped a concert, in front of a small invited audience, that was broadcast on MTV. It gave him a chance to display the strengths of his new music in an intimate setting.

After his marriage to Patti Scialfa, Springsteen said, "I realized my real life is waiting to be lived. All the love and the hope and the sorrow and the sadness—that's all over there, waiting to be lived."

Looking his 43 years but still lean and athletic, Springsteen put on a great performance. One of the highlights occurred when his wife, Patti, joined him on vocals for an emotionally charged version of "Human Touch." Columbia Records released 13 songs from the performance as *MTV UnPlugged,* a European-only limited edition live album. MTV also produced a one-hour documentary on Springsteen that featured rare film, photographs, and music from every part of his career, and a video of the show was released.

If Bruce Springsteen were to choose to retire today, he could look back with pride on a more than 20-year career in which he produced as much important music as any performer in rock and roll history. In all likelihood, however, he will continue his evolution as an artist and will offer his own brand of powerful and sincere music for many years to come.

In his 1992 interview with *Rolling Stone,* Springsteen said, "I feel like I'm at the peak of my creative powers right now. I think that in my work I'm presenting a complexity of ideas that I've been struggling to get to in the past. And it took me ten years of hard work outside of the music to get to this place. Real hard work. But when I got here, I didn't find bitterness and disillusionment. I found friendship and hope and faith in myself and a sense of purpose and passion. And it feels good."

Discography ★ ★ ★ ★ ★ ★ ★ ★ ★ ★ ★ ★ ★ ★ ★ ★ ★

(Albums and release dates)

Greetings from Asbury Park, N.J. (1/73)

The Wild, the Innocent and the E Street Shuffle (11/73)

Born To Run (8/75)

Darkness on the Edge of Town (6/78)

The River (10/80)

Nebraska (9/82)

Born in the U.S.A. (6/84)

Live/1975–1985 (11/86)

Tunnel of Love (10/87)

Human Touch (3/92)

Lucky Town (3/92)

MTV UnPlugged (no U.S. release)

Further Reading ★ ★ ★ ★ ★ ★ ★ ★ ★ ★ ★ ★ ★ ★

Eliot, Mark, with Mike Appel. *Down Thunder Road: The Making of Bruce Springsteen.* New York: Simon & Schuster, 1992.

Gillett, Charlie. *The Sound of the City.* New York: Pantheon, 1983.

Guralnick, Peter. *Sweet Soul Music.* New York: Harper & Row, 1986.

Hammond, John. *John Hammond on Record.* New York: Penguin, 1977.

Hillburn, Robert. *Springsteen.* New York: Rolling Stone Press/Scribner's, 1985.

Lynch, Kate. *Springsteen: No Surrender.* New York: Proteus, 1984.

Marcus, Greil. *Mystery Train.* New York: Dutton, 1982.

Marsh, Dave. *Born To Run: The Bruce Springsteen Story.* New York: Doubleday Dolphin, 1979.

———. *Glory Days: Bruce Springsteen in the 1980s.* New York: Pantheon, 1987.

Miller, Jim, ed. *The Rolling Stone Illustrated History of Rock and Roll.* New York: Rolling Stone/Random House, 1976.

Norman, Philip. *Shout! The Beatles in Their Generation.* New York: Simon & Schuster, 1981.

Weinberg, Max, with Robert Santelli. *The Big Beat.* Chicago: Contemporary, 1984.

Chronology ★ ★ ★ ★ ★ ★ ★ ★ ★ ★ ★ ★ ★ ★ ★ ★ ★

1949	Born Bruce Frederick Springsteen on September 23 in Freehold, New Jersey
1965	Auditions for and is rejected by a group called the Castiles; returns the next night after learning five guitar leads and is accepted into the band
1967	Graduates from high school in June; the Castiles break up
1968	Meets Southside Johnny and Steve Van Zandt; forms Steel Mill
1971	Disbands Steel Mill and forms the Bruce Springsteen Band; meets Clarence Clemons
1972	Signs contract with Mike Appel's production company, Laurel Canyon, which cuts a deal with Columbia Records; records first album, *Greetings from Asbury Park, N.J.*
1975	Releases *Born To Run,* coproduced by Jon Landau, and the album becomes an immediate hit; Springsteen appears on the covers of *Time* and *Newsweek* simultaneously
1976	Sues Mike Appel and Laurel Canyon for fraud and other illegalities; a court injunction prevents Springsteen from recording for a year
1977	The lawsuit is settled out of court and Springsteen is freed from his contracts with Appel; Landau becomes his manager and producer
1979	Participates in MUSE concerts
1980	*The River* is released; the band embarks on a sold-out U.S. tour
1981	Performs a benefit concert for the Vietnam Veterans of America that raises nearly $250,000
1982	Releases *Nebraska,* a solo album he originally recorded at home as a demo tape

1984	*Born in the U.S.A,* one of the top-selling albums of all time, is released
1985	Marries actress and model Julianne Phillips
1988	Divorces wife; participates in the Human Rights Now! tour
1990	Patti Scialfa gives birth to Springsteen's son, Evan James Springsteen, on July 25
1991	Springsteen marries Patti Scialfa in April; the couple's second child, Jessica Rae, is born on December 30
1992	Albums *Human Touch* and *Lucky Town* are released on the same day; Springsteen tours the United States and Europe without the E Street Band

Index ★★★★★★★★★★★★★★★★★★★★★★★★★★★

"All or Nothin' at All," 119
Amnesty International, 115
Appel, Mike, 44, 45, 46, 47, 48, 51, 52, 53, 54, 56, 59, 63, 64, 68, 69, 72, 73, 74, 79, 81, 113
  legal disputes, 83–88
Asbury Jukes, the, 76, 87
Asbury Park, New Jersey, 29, 30, 33, 35, 36, 39, 42, 43, 55, 64, 106, 116
  music scene, 20–31, 33–34, 39–43, 106

"Badlands," 90
"Because the Night," 114
"Better Days," 119
Bittan, Roy, 69, 75, 79, 105, 118, 119
"Blinded by the Light," 56, 59
"Bobby Jean," 106
Bonds, Gary "U.S.," 92
Born in the U.S.A., 103–6, 107, 108, 111, 114
"Born in the U.S.A.," 104, 105
Born To Run, 74–79, 83, 84, 86, 90, 94, 113
"Born To Run," 71, 73, 79
Born To Run (Marsh), 90
"Brilliant Disguise," 115
Bruce Springsteen Band, The, 39, 40

"Cadillac Ranch," 92
Carter, Ernest "Boom," 69
Castiles, the, 23–27, 29, 31, 96
CBS Records, 60, 63, 74, 80, 84
Clemons, Clarence, 11, 41, 42, 44, 55, 57, 65, 79, 80, 118

Columbia Records, 46, 48, 49, 51, 52, 54, 57, 58, 59, 60, 63, 64, 66, 70, 71, 73, 74, 76, 83, 84, 85, 88, 101, 120
Cretecos, Jim, 44, 45, 51, 56, 68

"Dancing in the Dark," 104, 105
Darkness on the Edge of Town, 89–91, 95
"Darkness on the Edge of Town," 90
Dr. Zoom and the Sonic Boom, 40, 41, 42, 43
Dylan, Bob, 23, 47, 48, 49, 58

Earth, 30, 32, 34
E Street Band, 11, 15, 66, 67, 76, 79, 80, 86, 89, 94, 95, 99, 103, 106, 114, 115, 116, 119
"E Street Shuffle, The," 64

Federici, Danny, 34, 55, 64
"Fever, The," 87
"Fire," 114
"For You," 56
"4th of July, Asbury Park (Sandy)," 64
Freehold, New Jersey, 17, 18, 23, 24, 25, 27

"Glory Days," 106
Greetings From Asbury Park, N.J., 55–58, 59, 63, 64, 66, 80
"Growin' Up," 56
Guthrie, Woody, 99, 113

Haines, Bart, 31, 96

Hammond, John, 46, 47–48, 49, 51, 52, 58, 60–61, 86
"Highway Patrolman," 102
Human Touch, 118, 119
"Human Touch," 119, 120

"Incident on 57th Street," 64
"Independence Day," 92
"It's Hard To Be a Saint in the City," 49

Jersey Shore, the, 27
"Jungleland," 79

Kovic, Ron, 95, 96

Landau, Jon, 69, 70, 74, 81, 84, 85, 86, 94
  as Springsteen's record producer, 75, 87, 89, 91, 100, 101, 113
Laurel Canyon, Ltd., 45, 51, 53, 57, 66, 68, 69, 83, 84, 86, 88
"Leap of Faith," 119
Live/1975–85, 113–14
Lofgren, Nils, 106
Lopez, Vini, 34, 39, 42, 55, 69, 80
Lucky Town, 118, 119

"Man's Job," 119
MTV Unplugged, 120
Musicians United for Safe Energy (MUSE), 91
"My Beautiful Reward," 119
"My Hometown," 103

Nebraska, 99–103, 104, 108, 111
"Nebraska," 101, 102

New Jersey, 17, 32, 36, 37, 41, 44, 45, 95, 108
New York City, 27, 37, 42, 44, 53, 74, 76, 77, 95, 99
No Nukes, 92
"No Surrender," 106

"Out in the Street," 92

Phillips, Julianne (first wife), 109–10, 111, 115
"Point Blank," 92
Presley, Elvis, 20, 21, 114
"Promised Land, The," 90

River, The, 92, 101, 103
Rogues, the, 23
Rolling Stone (magazine), 66, 69, 90, 118, 121
"Rosalita (Come Out Tonight)," 65, 91

Sancious, David, 39, 42, 55, 65, 69
Scialfa, Patti (second wife), 106, 116, 119, 120
"Sherry Darling," 92
Southside Johnny, 33, 35, 40, 76, 87, 103, 106
"Spirit in the Night," 12, 14, 56, 59
Springsteen, Adele (mother), 18, 20, 21, 22
Springsteen, Bruce Frederick albums, 92, 94, 99–103, 104–6, 107, 108, 109,

110, 113–115, 118–19, 120
appears on covers of *Time* and *Newsweek,* 81
and the Asbury Park music scene, 29–42
auditions for John Hammond, 48–49, 55
benefit concerts and records, 91–92, 95–97, 109, 115
birth, 18
childhood, 18–27
children, 117
divorce, 115
early bands, 23–27, 30–31, 32, 34–37, 39–43
education, 20, 23, 27, 32, 94
and the E Street Band, 11–15, 54–115, 119
friendship with Jon Landau, 69–70, 75, 84–85, 88, 94
legal dispute with Laurel Canyon, Ltd., 83–88
live performances, 11–15, 19, 60, 61, 67, 91, 94–95, 96–97, 107, 113–14, 120, 121
marriages, 109, 117
signs with Laurel Canyon Productions, 45, 51–52

Springsteen, Douglas (father), 18, 19, 20, 22, 32, 43

Tallent, Garry, 39, 42, 44, 55
"Tenth Avenue Freeze-out," 75, 76
Theiss, George, 23, 24, 25, 26
"Thundercrack," 71
"Thunder Road," 75, 78, 79
"Ties that Bind, The," 92
Tunnel of Love, 114–115
"Two Hearts," 92

Upstage, the, 33, 34, 35

Van Zandt, Steve, 33, 35, 39, 41, 42, 44, 55, 75, 76, 80, 87, 91, 103, 106, 109
Vietnam Veterans of America (VVA), 96, 97
Vietnam War, 31, 95, 96, 97, 105
Vinyard, Tex, 23–25, 26

Weinberg, Max, 69, 80, 105
West, Tinker, 35, 36, 37, 44, 45
Wild, the Innocent and the E Street Shuffle, The, 64–67, 70

"You Can Look (But You Better Not Touch)," 92

Ron Frankl was born in New York City and is a graduate of Haverford College. He is the author of *Duke Ellington* and *Charlie Parker* in Chelsea House's BLACK AMERICANS OF ACHIEVEMENT series. Mr. Frankl first heard Bruce Springsteen's music in 1974, and his life has never been the same.

Leeza Gibbons is a reporter for and cohost of the nationally syndicated television program "Entertainment Tonight" and NBC's daily talk show "John & Leeza from Hollywood." A graduate of the University of South Carolina's School of Journalism, Gibbons joined the on-air staff of "Entertainment Tonight" in 1984 after cohosting WCBS-TV's "Two on the Town" in New York City. Prior to that, she cohosted "PM Magazine" on WFAA-TV in Dallas, Texas, and on KFDM-TV in Beaumont, Texas. Gibbons also hosts the annual "Miss Universe," "Miss U.S.A.," and "Miss Teen U.S.A." pageants, as well as the annual Hollywood Christmas Parade. She is active in a number of charities and has served as the national chairperson for the Spinal Muscular Atrophy Division of the Muscular Dystrophy Association; each September, Gibbons cohosts the National MDA Telethon with Jerry Lewis.